What's in This Book

As a nutritionist, I have traveled across the country and around the world, seeing firsthand how diet affects the way we feel. Time and time again, I have been struck with the important place that soups and salads have in a healthy, active lifestyle. When made lovingly and with only the freshest ingredients, soups and salads are low in calories, and high in minerals, vitamins, and much-needed fiber. And soups and salads are delicious, with so many variations possible that even the fussiest eater is pleased.

Here are the very best of my recipes. Collected throughout my journeys, each recipe shows you how to create a dish that is wholesome, satisfying, and truly delicious.

From the classic Green Salad to the exotic Picante de Huevos, my salads combine fresh ingredients that nourish the body while delighting the palate. For extra taste and nutrition, I have also included my favorite dressings.

My simple-to-make soup recipes will help you concoct both hearty and refreshing soups—soups that round out a meal, and soups that are a meal in themselves. I've even included recipes for my special therapeutic soups.

I hope that you will enjoy these recipes as much as I do, and that you will learn how to enhance all your meals with the good taste of fresh and natural soups and salads.

I wish you the best of health!

Dr. Bernard Jensen

DR. JENSEN'S

Real Soup & Salad Book

Dr. Bernard Jensen

AVERY PUBLISHING GROUP INC.

Garden City Park, New York

Cover Design: Martin Hochberg and Rudy Shur
Cover Photo: Murray Alcosser Studio
Original Illustrations: Vicki Hudon
In-House Editors: Jacqueline Balla, Joanne Abrams, and Cynthia J. Eriksen
Typesetting: Multifacit Graphics, Inc.

Photo Credits

Front and back photos between pages 18 and 19; and front and back photos between pages 98 and 99: Photos by Jan and John Belleme.

Front and back photos between pages 34 and 35: Photos by Bernard Jensen.

Front photo between pages 66 and 67: Photo by Frederic George.

Back photo between pages 66 and 67: Photo courtesy of Stephen Blauer.

Library of Congress Cataloging-in-Publication Data

Jensen, Bernard, 1908–
    [Real soup & salad cookbook]
    Dr. Jensen's real soup & salad cookbook / Bernard Jensen.
      p.   cm.
    Includes index.
    ISBN 0-89529-410-9
    1. Cookery (Natural foods) 2. Soups. 3. Salads. I. Title.
II. Title: Real soup and salad cookbook. III. Title: Dr. Jensen's
real soup and salad cookbook.
TX741.J46   1989
641.8'13—dc19   89-30557
                                                    CIP

Printed in the United States of America

10 9 8 7 6 5 4 3 2

Introduction

In a world where so much of our modern food is of the "instant microwave" variety, salads have remained quite aloof. In today's kitchens, the mothers of America can come up with a pushbutton meal in practically record time. Only Mr. Salad can't be made in a microwave.

You see, salads come to us from ancient times; from many places and from many cultures. What, really, are most Chinese dishes—consisting of bean sprouts, water chestnuts, pea pods—but hot salads? The return of the salad to the American diet is not only here, but (we hope) here to stay.

Few preparations in the area of food offer the opportunity for creativity that a salad does. Here, a little imagination is worth far more than a measuring cup with a slide rule attached. It has been said that a true salad reflects the mood of the person who prepared it.

I once spoke with Señor G. L. Nava in Mexico. It was at Nava's Caesar Restaurant that the famous "Caesar Salad" was invented. An interesting side light of our talk was that the salad was actually created during a temporary meat shortage in an attempt to find a substitute for a full meal. That was one of the reasons why raw egg was added, along with croutons. So imagination, plus necessity, served to create a salad whose fame has swept the world.

Every mother knows that fresh greens are good for her family. In a sense, upon adding lettuce, tomato, a slice of onion, or relish to a sandwich, she is adding salad. She, like Señor Nava, is rounding out what she knows her husband and children need in the way of nutrition.

Unanimous approval and agreement among nutritionists regarding the importance of salads in the human diet has made this area of food a dietetic doctrine. In 1977, a report entitled *Dietary Goals for the United States* was issued by the U.S. Senate Select Committee on Nutrition and Human Needs. This report encouraged people to increase their consumption of complex carbohydrates, such as fresh local vegetables, and to reduce their intake of saturated fat, cholesterol, and refined sugar. Such dietary modifications could reduce the risk of cancer and other chronic diseases. (In 1982, the National Academy of Sciences issued a similar report called *Diet, Nutrition and Cancer*.)

Any differences we may suggest in salad preparation are trivial when compared to the mineral supplements that are involved. Should the salad be eaten first? Frankly, my viewpoint is that it *should* be eaten first—as a digestive stimulant.

However, a "forgotten salad" in the refrigerator can easily serve as a dessert. A little fruit, a few nuts, a hint of orange juice—such garnishes can make this dish a delightful way to *end* a meal.

ORIGIN OF SALADS

Most people don't know that the word "salad" comes from the Latin word "sal," meaning "salt." In the days of Caesar, it was a common practice to sprinkle various spring greens with salt. Therefore, dishes of vegetables sprinkled with salt came to be known as salads.

But, salads were being eaten even before Roman times, although they were not called by that name. Evidence indicates that primitive man ate freely of sweet grass, pungent herbs, and savory weeds. The ancient Egyptians were skilled in the art of mixing oil, vinegar, and oriental spices, which they poured over their greens. The Greeks used salad as a final course—as a fresh, crisp finale after the sweets.

In Shakespeare's day, salads were regarded as tonics to be tasted at the approach of spring. In the eighteenth century, salad-making became a fashionable fad among the French nobility. In the elegant 80s, wealthy American hostesses imported chefs from France to create and to mix their elaborate salads.

Our great-grandmothers' salads usually consisted of cabbage slaw, pickled beets, and wilted lettuce with bacon drippings. By the turn of the century, salad's popularity lagged. Until fairly recent years, cookbooks had little to offer in the way of salad-making.

Now there is another surge in the popularity of the salad. Once regarded as a mere garnish on the plate or a fancy decoration for the banquet table, today salad provides the finishing touch to almost any meal.

THE MAKING OF A GOOD SALAD

A salad is no better than the greens that go into it. Salad greens should always be garden-fresh and free from blemishes and sprays. They should be carefully washed in cold running water, then shaken gently to remove any excess moisture. Slight dampness helps to keep the greens fresh and crisp during storage, but too much moisture shortens their life span. Vegetables should either be placed in the refrigerator hydrator in a clear plastic bag or wrapped in a clean cloth until ready to use.

Lemon juice, or the remainder of the dressing, may be added when the salad is ready to serve.

Salads are known for their health value all over the world. They form an important part of the diets of health-minded people everywhere. In this book you'll find not only favorite recipes used in our own country, but a special section devoted to salad recipes from friends around the world.

Hints for Selecting Salad Greens

Select only fresh young greens. By greens, I mean lettuce, celery, cabbage, chives, chicory leaves, beet tops, endive, escarole, and sprouts. Greens provide the foundation for the basic tossed green salad. My list of greens isn't, of course, exhaustive. Spinach leaves, chard, wild miner's lettuce, dandelion greens (be especially sure they're fresh), and coriander leaves are also excellent additions. By selecting fresh young greens from this list, you'll be getting the most flavor and tenderness for your money—as well as the most nutritional value.

- Celery should have clean, thick stalks with fresh, green leaves. Avoid limp celery with wilted or brown leaves.
- Cabbage should be heavy for its size, with a firm, crisp head.
- Chives should be bright green, and in tufts.
- Chicory leaves should be broad, with curly edges.
- Beet tops should be fresh and small, from young beets.
- Endive should be curly, in bunchy green heads with yellow-green centers. Belgian endive has smooth, yellow-white elongated heads.
- Escarole is like curly endive, but has broader leaves. It may be either blanched or green.
- Sprouts include alfalfa, almonds, lentils, mung beans, sesame, sunflower, and wheat. These particular sprouts are the easiest to grow, delicious, and most versatile.

Lettuce comes in heads of different varieties, some of which are: Boston, butter, leaf, and romaine. Most types have tender, delicate leaves, but romaine has long, wide leaves of dark green, and has a sturdier texture. Both the inner light green leaves and outer dark green leaves are good for salad. The darker, tougher, stronger-flavored greens (such as escarole, chicory, parsley, watercress, and romaine) are richer in minerals and vitamins than milder-flavored greens.

If you need to enliven your salads, try rosemary and tarragon (but be sparing). Some supermarkets now carry fresh herbs if you don't grow your own. Fresh herbs are milder than dried herbs and are more fun to use.

Regardless of its size, a salad can be made with a mixture of different garden vegetables. Sliced radishes, shredded carrots, and grated parsnips add crunch and zest to a dinner salad. Use your imagination. To whet a child's appetite for a salad, add raisins or pineapple bits and use a mild, sweet dressing (like French). Also, try using raw zucchini and raw asparagus, straight from the garden.

It helps to have a wooden salad bowl large enough to allow tossing and mixing without spilling. Salad tongs and a large wooden salad fork and spoon for tossing and serving are standard equipment. A pair of kitchen scissors is useful for cutting up parsley and onion tops and for halving grapes. Your favorite gadgets for scraping, coring, shredding, and curling will also come in handy.

SOUPS! SOUPS! SOUPS!

Like salads, soups are universally enjoyed and are builders of health. While salads tend to be hot-weather foods, soup is more of a cold-weather favorite.

The first soups may have been created, according to anthropologists, not long after prehistoric man tamed fire (around 500,000 B.C.). Prehistoric cooks boiled meat and vegetables in stone potholes by heating small rocks and tossing them into the pothole with water, meat, roots, seeds, and vegetables, until the concoction was cooked to their liking.

Stone cooking pots found in Central America date back to 7,000 B.C., while pottery was developed around 6,000 B.C. Both made possible a more convenient way of making soups, although some cultures used turtle shells or hollow sections of bamboo to heat soups—perhaps even before 7,000 B.C.

Soups are mentioned in the earliest writings known to man. Bean and rice soup, specifically, was described in a first-century manuscript from India. A Chinese poem from the third century referred to soup. Before Columbus sailed to America, the Indians were making soup.

The HANES Report (Health and Nutritional Evaluation Service), a governmental study conducted by the Department of Health and Human Services, came up with some interesting findings in 1973 (the report was updated in the late seventies, and a HANES 3 is currently in the works). This nutritional survey of American eating habits arrived at the conclusion that the healthiest people are those who consume large amounts of dairy products and soup. The study goes on to say that this is largely because those who eat a lot of soup are less overweight, since it is both low in calories and high in nutrients.

Don't wait for winter to investigate some new soup ideas. Soup can be an all-year favorite once you become familiar with the many varieties of "iced soup." Don't forget nutritious raw soups, either warm or cold, as well as all those hot cheering varieties. There is a soup to meet almost every need. Whet the appetite with a light consommé, make soups thick with vegetables to bring up your vegetable quota, serve a rich bean or pea soup to satisfy protein requirements—in fact, soup can be made so thick and hearty that it can become a meal in itself.

What Makes a Good Soup?

When making soups, be sure you don't boil the life out of your vegetables. Just simmer them. Even if you are including barley or rice in your brew, give these a preliminary cooking and, when nearly tender, add the vegetables so that they only cook for twenty minutes or so. Overcooking is one reason why people have to season soups so strongly. Conservatively cooked vegetables will retain their true flavor. Extra spark can be supplied with a little vegetable seasoning, herbs, garlic, a dash of soy sauce, or a vegetable bouillon cube on occasion. A small amount of butter stirred in after cooking is also nice.

For those who cannot tolerate coarse bulk, a cooked soup can often be liquefied instead of strained. In this way, much of the vegetable value is not lost. A little cream, raw milk, or nut milk added at the end of the cooking will convert almost any soup into a rich, creamy mixture for variety and broader nutritional value.

Soup can be made with liquids other than water. Oat straw tea, a bland tea high in silicon, builds nerves, skin, hair, and nails. Other herb teas can also be incorporated. For example, mint teas add flavor to your soup and are therapeutic; alfalfa and comfrey are also excellent. Bran water is a good mineralizing base from which to start your soup. Always add any water left over after cooking vegetables to your stockpot. Instead of discarding the outside leaves, tough stalks, and stems of vegetables, simmer these in plenty of water and strain off this broth for a valuable soup base. A vegetable bouillon cube or vegetable powder will make this into a rich consommé of its own.

I do not generally use meat stock. Meat cooked in water makes the kidneys' job that much harder. All meat should be broiled, baked, or roasted. However, my Veal Joint Broth, the highest sodium broth

around, is made from a clean, uncut, fresh veal joint. This is excellent for keeping joints limber and the stomach, glands, and digestive tract in good order. Other special broths and soups for health are dealt with in the recipe section. I value my neutral Potato Peeling Broth so highly, I use it far more often than fruits for increasing elimination and reducing fever.

Lentils, beans, and dried peas are very nutritious, and should be a regular part of the diet. Many people avoid these because of the resulting gas. The hulls, however, are responsible for this. If pre-soaking and long cooking do not soften these enough for you, make a purée and strain the hulls right out. This will enable even the most delicate digestive system to handle legume soups very nicely. For extra nutrition and digestibility, sprout whole peas and beans before preparation. This reduces their starchy nature and increases their vitamin value.

Never use flour thickening for soups. A little arrowroot is fine, but it is much better to fill your soups with vegetables, or use a little rice or barley (or wheat germ or flaxseed meal after cooking) to absorb any excess liquid. Serve with a dash of raw cream.

Most people have a tendency to serve soups either too hot or too cold. Very hot food causes a flacidity of tissues which hampers digestion, while the same result occurs from iced foods because these contract the tissues, preventing the proper flow of digestive juices. So serve "iced" soups cool, but not icy, and adjust hot soups to a comfortable serving temperature.

Don't forget your garnish. Appearance can add much to the enjoyment of a dish—and your garnish can also be nutritious in the bargain. Quite often the usual parsley can be waived in favor of chopped watercress or chives, alfalfa sprouts, a grated carrot or beet, or thinly-sliced radishes or cucumber. Even chopped nuts and shredded hard boiled egg offer a surprising change.

It's a good idea to save any extra soup and freeze it in cubes (stored in plastic bags). When in a hurry for a warming beverage, you can simply heat up three or four cubes. Soup is one of the greatest international foods—universally loved, nourishing, comforting, strengthening, and as varied as the imagination of its maker.

As a final note, I'd like to mention that in making homemade soup it is all too easy to keep on adding tasty ingredients, until the soup is so full of solids that it is more like a goulash or stew than a soup. Of course, you may want a very thick concentration of solids in an occasional soup. But if you get to the point during soup-making where you have *too many* solids, be sure to add more vegetable stock, broth, or water. This should be done as early as possible to allow the new liquid to develop flavor.

Important Tips

Soups and salads are delicious and healthful additions to any menu. To maximize the taste and nutritional value of these dishes, be sure to keep the following guidelines in mind.

- Buy only unsprayed fruits and vegetables. Organically grown produce will give you the best flavor and the greatest nutrient content, and will do so *without* harmful chemical residues.

- Use only the freshest fruits and vegetables at their peak of ripeness. Fresh produce not only tastes better than immature or overripe produce, but also is nutritionally superior.

- As often as possible, make "rainbow" salads. By eating salads of many different colors, you not only will be sure to get all the vitamins and minerals you need, but also will enliven your meals and help to create greater energy and harmony within the body.

- Be sure to use only cold-pressed oils. When possible, choose virgin cold-pressed olive oil. Other good oils include safflower, sesame seed, soybean, sunflower, avocado, and apricot kernel oil.

- When making soups, always stir in cream, milk, and butter either at the table or just before serving. Never heat these ingredients, as heat will destroy many of their healthful properties.

- Don't boil the life out of your vegetables. To preserve color, flavor, and nutrients, keep your soups at a simmer, and leave ingredients a little chewy.

- Be sure to eat 60 percent of your food raw every day. This will insure your getting enough fiber to keep the bowel toned, healthy, and active.

- We each have our own preferences. Don't be afraid to adjust a recipe—changing proportions, substituting ingredients, and varying seasonings—until you find what you like best.

1. BEAUTIFUL SALADS:
Why Are They So Popular?

AN INTRODUCTION TO SALADS

In recent years, salads have become increasingly popular, and have begun to take up more space on most restaurant menus. Many restaurants—even fast-food chains—now have salad bars where you can make your own salad with whatever dressing or garnishes you prefer.

Why have salads become such an attractive item on the menu? Health-conscious Americans have become more aware of the benefits of salads in their diets as a result of reports like the National Academy of Sciences' *Diet, Nutrition, and Cancer* (1982) and more recent studies, which indicate that dietary imbalances are among the reasons why our national rates of cancer and cardiovascular disease are so high. Such studies recommend a higher intake of salads, vegetables, fruits, and whole grain cereals, and suggest that we eat less meat.

Another reason for the salad craze in the United States is our nation's rediscovery of fitness and its love affair with slender, youthful bodies. Reducing diets, for better or worse (mostly worse, in my view), have become extremely popular. Salads fit right in with all of this—fitness, slenderness, dieting, and health consciousness.

A SALAD'S NUTRITIONAL VALUE

I consider salad the most important part of any meal. Why? Because it is freshly made with "live" foods that have been recently picked. Our food should be our medicine, because what we eat is eventually transformed into tissue-building materials. Salads are health builders. They are loaded with vitamins, minerals, live enzymes, and prostaglandins (the hormone-like substances that aid hormones in their effects on body cells).

Chlorophyll, the "plant blood" of all green vegetables, is the most effective cleanser found in nature. Green vegetables are rich in this, just as they are rich in vitamins, minerals, and prostaglandins. Greens help the body to assimilate iron and are also powerful blood builders.

I once cared for a patient with pernicious anemia and built up her red blood count from 3,000,000 to 4,500,000 in a matter of three months. How? By using greens. Chlorophyll, together with the iron found in most green plants, is the best blood builder we can put into our bodies. Where's the best place to get these greens? You guessed it—in a salad. Nothing is better for the repair, rebuilding, and rejuvenation of cell structure.

There is also no better source of fiber than a salad. Whether you get your fiber from sprouts, seeds, beans, celery, lettuce, endive, or squash, you will receive the roughage necessary to move the bowel contents along at the proper rate and to help tone the muscles of the bowel wall.

In addition to providing iron and fiber, a salad containing raw vegetables is a good source of iodine. In contrast to raw salads, cooked vegetables lose part of their nutritional value. For example, when you cook any iodine-containing food, the iodine is partly lost in the cooking water. In fact, vegetables cooked in water lose virtually all of their iodine. This trace element is necessary for the thyroid gland to regulate the body's metabolism.

Another important element found in salad vegetables is fluorine. Fluorine is a cleanser, germicide, and bone and tooth strengthener. Germs can't survive in the presence of fluorine. That's why the artificially-synthesized laboratory fluorine in toothpaste is so popular. But fluorine is needed not only for the teeth—we need it for our entire body to help prevent disease. Salad vegetables are the best sources of the fluorine we need.

You might also like to add cucumbers to your salad, not just for their taste, but because they are so high in sodium. Sodium is cooling to the blood, and the cucumber's outer green covering is high in chlorophyll. Sodium is necessary for the joints and gastrointestinal system. The bowel wall cannot work without it. The stomach wall needs it. Your joints must have it in order to prevent uric acid from settling there, and for flexibility. Eating cucumber seeds is one of the best things you can do for the intestinal tract. Strawberries are also among the foods high in sodium and can be added to your fruit salad. Black Mission figs are high in this element as well.

For a good source of the element potassium, you might add watercress to your salad. Watercress is the absolute highest in potassium. Potassium is a great alkalinizer for the body. It also assists kidney activity and helps eliminate water for those who are edemic and overweight.

THE IMPORTANCE OF VARIETY

It's necessary for every salad to have a variety of vegetables. I don't think any salad can feed the whole body unless it contains at least six to eight different vegetables. Don't forget—you want to use foods that will build up the entire body.

By eating a rainbow salad—a salad of many different-colored vegetables—you will be doing your body the greatest amount of good, and will rebuild every organ and tissue. The red beet, for instance, is helpful for moving bile through the gallbladder and liver. The green leafy vegetables (chlorophyll) in your salad will act as body deodorizers. Adding a little orange carrots to your salad will protect your body from infection because of their carotene content.

In addition to these vegetables, you need yellow laxative foods. Why are some people always constipated? Because they don't eat right. Have you ever considered using corn in your salad? Fresh corn right from the cob—yellow corn—is good for constipation and is one of the best foods for growing children.

Like all yellow fruits, squash is laxative. By including more of these in salads, bowel trouble can be largely eliminated, especially in children. You might want to try different types of raw squashes in your salad. Raw grated zucchini, grated yellow crookneck, and summer squash are all delicious additions.

THE BENEFITS OF RAW FOODS

When making a salad, you may want to cook some vegetables—turnips, for instance—before combining them with the raw vegetables. However, because cooking foods often depletes them of their nutrients, it is best to eat most vegetables raw. The American Cancer Society now states that vegetables are an aid in lowering the risk of cancer. So raw vegetables should be eaten every day. I recommend eating about 60 percent of your food raw every day. When you consume this amount of raw food, you are getting enough fiber to keep the bowel toned, healthy, and active. Eating salads is a good way to satisfy this requirement. How much salad should you have? It's a good idea to eat one big salad a day, or to have two smaller vegetable salads, perhaps at noon and evening meals.

Some people can take more raw foods than others. At first you may have to wilt the vegetables or have them liquefied, but eventually you'll be able to handle them.

Now, the purest, softest, and easiest way of getting nutrition from raw vegetables when you can't eat them whole is through their juices. And the best vegetable juice to use as a base is carrot juice. You can always add a little parsley juice, beet juice, escarole juice, or any of the green leafy lettuce juices if you like.

Because of the liquid contained in raw vegetable juices, you won't have to drink as much water. Since this vegetable juice is "triturated," as the homeopaths would say, it has just the right amount of the necessary chemical elements that can most easily be assimilated by the body.

The nutritional value of raw vegetables is better than that of cooked vegetables. So why not go on a raw diet? Hippocrates, the father of medicine, once said that extreme measures may have to be taken in the case of extreme disease conditions. However, few people go to the proper food extremes to build and benefit their health.

I've put many patients on a diet of raw vegetables, juices, and liquefied raw foods in order to bring back the minerals depleted from the body through years of unbalanced diets. But always keep in mind that an extreme diet should be followed only under the supervision of a doctor or nutritionist, for it can be dangerous.

SALAD ADDITIONS

In addition to nutritious vegetables, there are many other things you can do to spice up salads. How about adding whole grain macaroni, spaghetti, and other pastas? Of course, you should get the best of these. There is artichoke flour that is made into pasta, and spinach flour. Many pastas have vegetable fillings, and you might try these as well. Hearts of artichoke and hearts of palm are delicious additions to salads. Jerusalem artichoke can be added to salad too; it is very good for those people who cannot digest starchy foods well. You might also like grated macadamia nuts, sliced almonds, or a pinch of fresh coconut. More exotic additions include rose petals, nasturtium leaves, and nasturtium petals. Hibiscus flowers have been used in salads for many years. What's your pleasure?

You can use young or old beets, and young or old carrots. You can't do the same with fruits, however, because they must be mature for full flavor and nutritional value. You can't eat a green apricot or a rotten one—it must be ripe.

Ripe fruits will feed the body properly; green fruits will not. Immature fruits will not feed it properly. This is why I recommend eating six vegetables and only two fruits each day.

There are many seasonings that can be put on salads. There is a broth powder made up of dehydrated vegetables that can be used. Onions can be added for those that like them. Chives can be added, as can many herbs like thyme, rosemary, and hazel. Anise and marjoram make a wonderful combination. Experiment to find which seasonings you like best.

THE FOUNDATION OF THE SALAD: LETTUCE AND OTHER GREENS

Because lettuce is generally considered the base of a salad, it is helpful to differentiate between the various kinds. I prefer using only lettuce varieties with deep green leaves. They are high in chlorophyll, which is so necessary for cleansing the body.

Compared with other types of lettuce, iceberg lettuce is relatively low in nutritional value. It is practically devoid of chlorophyll, being composed mostly of water. While this type of lettuce is not harmful, I'd use less of it in salads and larger amounts of romaine lettuce and butter lettuce.

In addition to these varieties of lettuce, you may also use spinach leaves for your salad base. Many restaurants offer raw spinach salad, which is relatively low in oxalic acid. When any food containing oxalic acid is cooked, the amount of oxalic acid is doubled. This hinders calcium assimiliation. Oxalic acid, therefore, can contribute to joint pains and problems. So spinach is best consumed raw in salads. I don't recommend using spinach juice, though, because it, too, is high in oxalic acid.

Use all the greens you can in your salad—Belgian endive, escarole, watercress, parsley, and even the tops of celery. Beet or turnip greens are also good. You don't have to use much to derive their benefits.

BEWARE OF SPRAYED FRUITS AND VEGETABLES

Although fresh fruits and vegetables are an essential part of the diet, we should beware of sulfite sprays, such as those sometimes used on salad bar vegetables in order to keep them looking fresh. After several deaths over the last few years due to sulfite sprays, the government stepped in to regulate their use. However, sprays probably caused more allergy disturbances than anything else.

Last year, 10 million watermelons were destroyed in California because of toxic sprays that are absorbed in the intestines. There's an arsenic spray used on celery that sometimes makes it unfit for human consumption as well.

Many people have a glass of wine with meals. They don't realize that wine, too, often contains toxic spray residues. In fact, I was in central California where some fifty-two ranches grow grapes for use by wineries, and only three of the growers grew grapes without using toxic spray. This is where much of our trouble originates. Poison residues have been found on many vegetables and fruits. Because sprays are used on fruit trees while they are in blossom, bees get into it, and the spray often ends up in our honey as well.

Not all salad vegetables are sprayed. For instance, watercress, parsley, and escarole are safe to eat, and you should use more of them. They are three of the finest vegetables around. Unfortunately, those vegetables that are sprayed are the ones that we consume the most.

Sprays used on our food crops have increased many health risks, producing taints in the body that encourage disease. Toxic sprays are even more dangerous than drugs. You can become a miasmic patient—one who is difficult to heal—because spray residues become imbedded in your body tissues. Always wash all vegetables and fruits carefully.

SALAD DRESSINGS

You will not enjoy your salad unless you find the right dressing. You might experiment by adding oils, nut butters, apple cider, vinegar, buttermilk or avocados—to mention only a few ingredients. I recommend using expeller-pressed oils (also called cold-pressed oils) instead of solvent-extracted oils, which are less flavorful and sometimes contain solvent residue. Expeller-pressed oils are available in health food stores. Some of the best varieties include olive, safflower, sesame seed, soybean, sunflower, avocado, and apricot kernel oil.

I like to use natural apple cider vinegar for my salad, as well as good quality wine vinegar. Herbal vinegar can be made by steeping fresh herbs in natural apple cider vinegar. (See pages 77 and 159.)

MAKING SALADS APPETIZING FOR CHILDREN

Because of their nutritional value, salads should not be limited to adults; children can also benefit from a good salad. Of course, Popeye has helped to popularize spinach with kids, but there are other salad vegetables that children should also have.

I myself did not like salads as a child, but I found that a handful of steamed raisins tossed into the salad made it a lot more attractive. I would eat my salad in order to get the raisins. Children might also enjoy cut-up dates or figs, or stewed fruits that have been mixed in. Pineapple makes a tasty addition to salads. Sometimes a sweet dressing will help, too, until kids develop a taste for raw vegetables.

Parsnips can be finely shredded and used in a salad. Shredded carrots make a wonderful base in salads for children. A good source of vitamin A, I think they should be a daily part of every child's diet.

Preparing School Lunches

When my children were in school, as a rule they never had bread unless they had vegetables along with it. In general, bread by itself can be very constipating. Most people have bread with every meal. Bread or other starches should never be eaten without a vegetable or some kind of fiber-rich food— like reconstituted dried fruits.

My children ate plenty of lettuce with nut butters and varieties of vegetables and vegetable fillings. Once when my son David was teased and called a "rabbit" by his classmates because of all the vegetables he brought for lunch, he replied, "At least I'm not a *constipated* rabbit."

If you don't make your own bread, you can purchase fresh bread from the bakery or get a fresh whole grain loaf, without preservatives, from a health food store.

Here are some of the sandwiches my children took to school:

- avocado and romaine on whole wheat or pumpernickel bread
- lettuce, grated carrot, and chopped raisin on date and nut bread
- dates and nuts on whole wheat bread
- romaine with celery and carrot, chopped fine
- nut spread with olives and chopped watercress on whole wheat date bread
- mashed banana with cashew nut spread, honey, or freshly grated coconut

Simple salads may put in a tightly-covered glass jar and eaten from the jar with a spoon or fork. Milk, nut or soy milk, and milk soups are important additions and should always be included. Once in a while, a custard, agar gelatin dessert, homemade health candy, or soaked dried fruits may be included as a final touch to a child's lunch.

A FINAL NOTE

Those people who regularly include good salads in their diets will usually find that they are in good health. Salads should be one of the mainstays of everyone's food regimen. I believe that soup and salad are the two things that every cook must know about. Nothing will keep you in better health than a good salad. A salad should comprise more than half the meal, to help provide the amount of raw foods that we need every day of our lives. In Chapter 2, I offer you my favorite salad recipes. Try them—maybe some of them will become your favorites too!

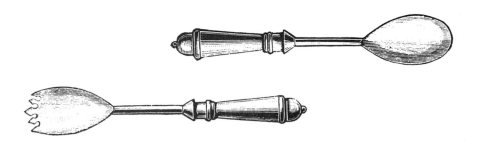

2. *MY FAVORITE SALADS:*
Health and Harmony for All Seasons

For most people, salads—and salad dressings—are an acquired taste (except for the dessert-like fruit salads that even children enjoy). But once you begin to enjoy tossed greens and other vegetable salads, it will be a life-long love affair. Unlike most cravings in life, you don't have to hold back if a sudden desire for a green salad begins to tempt your taste buds (provided that the dressing isn't loaded with calories). You have to watch those dressings, which I'll be talking about in Chapter 3. Fruit salads are usually higher in calories than vegetable salads, so you can't be quite as free to eat all you want, especially if nuts and grated coconut (high in fat) are included in the salad. The saving grace of most fruit salads is that they are rich enough—or sweet enough—to quench any desire to overeat.

The following cornucopia of salads includes my favorites—all taste-tested and time-proven. Plan on enjoying yourself as you pick and choose from these taste-tingling, health-building salad recipes from my own personal recipe collection. Also keep in mind that you are free to use a dressing of your choice if you don't agree with the ones I've selected. Once you become more familiar with herbs, you'll also discover that you can change the taste of your salad by varying the types and amounts of herbs used. Finally, serving amounts are based on the size of an ordinary dinner salad.

TOSSED GREEN SALAD— Variation I

SERVES 4

2 cups romaine
1/2 cup endive
1/2 cup watercress
1/4 cup chopped parsley
1 tsp. chopped tarragon
1/8 cup chopped chervil
1 tsp. chopped dill
Sour Cream or Yogurt Dressing (pages 75 and 76)

1. Arrange loosely-torn greens and herbs in a salad bowl.
2. Serve with Yogurt or Sour Cream Dressing.

TOSSED GREEN SALAD—Variation II

SERVES 4

1 cup escarole
1 cup romaine
1/2 cup young mustard greens
1/2 cup watercress
1/4 cup chopped chives
1 tsp. fennel spray
1 tsp. dill
2 tomatoes, wedged
French Dressing (page 71)

1. Combine the chopped greens and tomatoes.
2. Mix in French Dressing and toss.

Shaping Up Nicely

You can enhance the look of any salad simply by varying the way different vegetables are cut up. Round or diagonal, triangular or rectangular, half-moon or quartered slices—the list goes on and on. There's always plenty of room for creativity as you shape the individual slices, arrange them carefully on the dish, and add an attractive garnish.

Keep in mind that combining differently-shaped vegetables in your salad will create a unique look. Or you might decide to slice all your vegetables in one particular way. Whatever you choose, dinner guests and family members alike will be impressed by your imagination and your desire to prepare something really special just for them!

Cubes, dicing, and mincing

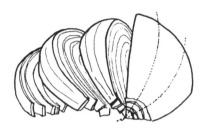

Wedge slices

Slicing big, leafy greens

Along the veins   **The stem**   **Slicing greens**

Slicing cabbages

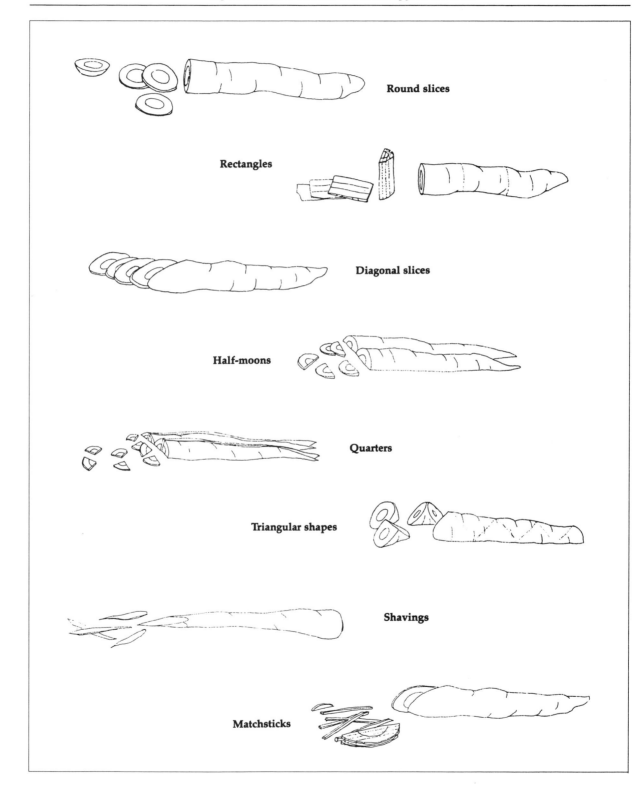

Round slices

Rectangles

Diagonal slices

Half-moons

Quarters

Triangular shapes

Shavings

Matchsticks

CHEF'S SALAD

SERVES 2

4 cups salad greens (romaine, endive, watercress, parsley)
2 tomatoes, wedged
½ cup chopped celery
½ cup grated cheddar cheese
1 hard boiled egg, chopped
French Dressing (page 71)

1. Arrange loosely-torn greens in a salad bowl.
2. Combine with celery, cheese, and egg.
3. Arrange wedged tomatoes around the bowl.
4. Serve with French Dressing.

CAESAR SALAD

SERVES 4-6

1 garlic clove, crushed
½ cup olive oil
Vegetable seasoning, to taste
1 egg, coddled for 1 minute
2 Tbs. lemon juice
½ cup grated Parmesan cheese
2 heads romaine
½ cup croutons (page 101)

1. Tear the romaine into bite-sized pieces and place in salad bowl.
2. Add olive oil that has been marinated overnight with the crushed garlic and toss well until the romaine is well coated.
3. Break the egg into the middle of the salad, add lemon juice and vegetable seasonings, and mix so the salad has a creamy look.
4. Toss in the grated cheese and mix again.
5. Add croutons and serve immediately.

BEAN SALAD

SERVES 4

2 cups salad greens
¼ cup chopped young onions
1½ cups cooked kidney beans (or canned, unsalted beans)
½ cup chopped celery
Oil and Vinegar or Vinaigrette Dressing (pages 77 and 78)

1. Combine greens, beans, and other vegetables in a salad bowl and toss lightly with Oil and Vinegar or Vinaigrette Dressing.
2. If liquid from canned kidney beans is used, no dressing is needed.

WATERCRESS SALAD

SERVES 4

2 cups watercress
1 small head Chinese cabbage
½ cup minced parsley
1 tomato, wedged
Choice of dressing

1. Shred the cabbage.
2. Combine the greens and tomato together in a salad bowl.
3. Toss with dressing of your choice.

CARROT AND MINT SALAD

SERVES 4-6

4 cups grated carrots
½ cup fresh grated coconut
2 tsp. minced mint leaves
½ cup slivered or ground almonds
10 ripe olives
Choice of dressing

1. Combine carrots, coconut, almonds, and mint.
2. Toss with dressing of your choice and garnish with olives.

SERVES 4

MINTED LETTUCE SALAD

2 heads butter lettuce
1/2 cup chopped mint leaves
4 tomatoes, wedged
Lemon and Honey Dressing (page 78)

1. Cut each lettuce head in half, and place on four salad plates.
2. Combine fresh mint leaves with Lemon and Honey Dressing.
3. Pour over lettuce wedges, garnish with tomatoes, and serve.

SERVES 4

COMBINATION SALAD—
Variation I

1 large head romaine
1 sliced cucumber
1 tomato, wedged
1/4 cup chopped green onions
1/2 cup fresh or cooked peas
Choice of dressing

1. Combine loosely-torn romaine and all vegetables in a salad bowl, mix well, and serve with your choice of dressing.

"We were created for joy!"

Combination Salad With Yellow Squash.

*"A long life is not good enough,
but a good life is long enough."*

Endive Salad.

All Greens Were Not Created Equal

Before tossing a salad together, it is important that you familiarize yourself with the basics—the types of greens from which you may choose. The following are the most common:

Romaine. This lettuce is probably the most strongly flavored, and is especially delicious with tomatoes and avocados. It is characterized by a long head and spoon-shaped leaves.

Leaf. Crisp and curly, this type of lettuce grows in large, leafy bunches.

Iceberg. Perhaps the most familiar lettuce, it is a compact head of light green leaves. Popularly cut in wedges or separated and made into a lettuce cup for holding potato or fruit salad, etc.

Curly endive or chicory. Leaves are thin and twisted, and are dark green at the edges and pale yellow at the heart. Delicious with grapefruit and orange sections or tomatoes.

Belgian endive. A straight and slender leaf, it can be eaten alone (like celery) or with other greens. It is often more than six inches in length.

Escarole. The "broad-leaf endive." Similar to chicory, with leaves that are less curly. They are dark green, with yellow edges.

Although not mentioned in this book, the following not-so-common varieties may be used in place of any of the above:

Radicchio. Although red in color, this delicious wild chicory from the Venetian province is still considered a "green." There are three types: the red Verona chicory (short leaves and roundish heart), the red Treviso chicory (long leaves and tapered heart), and the Castelfranco variegated chicory (green leaves speckled with red spots and streaks).

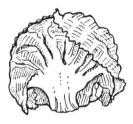

Arugula. A Mediterranean plant of the mustard family, much used in Italian kitchens and increasingly in America. Its pungent leaves may be used alone, producing a very strong-tasting salad, although most prefer to combine it with other greens such as Belgian endive. Also called *roquette*.

SERVES 4-6

COMBINATION SALAD—
Variation II

Olive oil (to taste)
Lemon juice (to taste)
Tomato sauce (to taste)
Honey (to taste)
Mashed garlic (to taste)
2 sliced tomatoes
1/2 cup cooked cut string beans
1/2 cup cooked lima beans
1/2 cup cucumber cubes
1/2 cup broccoli, broken into pieces
1 cup radish slices
1/2 cup sliced mushrooms
1 cup raw, grated carrots
3 cups mixed greens
French Dressing (page 71)

1. Combine vegetables and greens and toss lightly with olive oil, lemon juice, tomato sauce, honey, and mashed garlic (to taste).
2. A clove of garlic may be added to the French Dressing and allowed to stand in a glass container overnight to give a garlic flavor, if so desired.
3. Toss with French Dressing and serve.

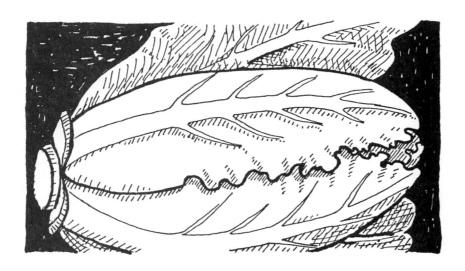

CODDLED EGG SALAD

SERVES 4

1 head romaine
1 cup bread, cut into small cubes
2 eggs, coddled for 1 minute
1 sliver mashed garlic
½ cup grated cheddar cheese
1 Tbs. soy sauce
1 Tbs. butter or olive oil
French Dressing (page 71)

Please note that in this and other recipes calling for olive oil, any vegetable oils (preferably cold-pressed), such as safflower, sesame seed, soybean, sunflower, avocado, or apricot kernel oil, may be used.

1. Wash, drain, and break romaine into pieces. Place in salad bowl.
2. Heat butter (or oil) with garlic and sauté the bread cubes until golden brown.
3. Mix with romaine.
4. Break the coddled eggs into a small dish and add the soy sauce, grated cheese, and dressing.
5. Pour over salad and toss lightly.

SERVES 2-4

CABBAGE SALAD
(Cole Slaw)

1 cup shredded green cabbage
1 cup shredded red cabbage
1 cup shredded Chinese cabbage or celery
1 cup mayonnaise (pages 73–74)
¼ cup fresh cream
Honey (to taste)
Orange slices (optional)

Cabbage salad can be varied, using grated carrots, raisins, and coconut, or other harmonizing vegetables, fruits, or nuts. Avocado strips, tomato wedges, or artichoke hearts may also be added for garnish and taste appeal.

1. Combine the shredded cabbage with mayonnaise, honey, and cream.
2. Orange slices may be placed on top for color.

SERVES 6

FRESH CORN SALAD

5 cups raw corn, removed from cob
1 cup fresh grated coconut
2 cups green lettuce
½ cup green pepper, cut into thin strips
Coconut Dressing (page 79)

Coconut milk is the liquid found in the coconut. If you can't obtain a coconut, though, buy canned unsweetened coconut milk or mix unsweetened coconut milk powder with water.

1. Combine corn with grated coconut and lettuce.
2. Toss with Coconut Dressing, and garnish with strips of green pepper. (Pimento strips may also be used as garnish.)

SALAD TRAY
(For Patio Party)

Slices of firm tomatoes
Sliced green pepper
Cucumber slices
Thin carrot strips
Crisp radishes
Cauliflower clusters
Watercress
Parsley
Various dressings

Amounts will vary, depending upon the number of guests.

1. On a large, oblong serving tray, arrange assorted vegetables in single rows running the width of the tray.
2. In one row place tomatoes; in the next row rings of green pepper.
3. Follow this with a row of cucumber slices, then a row of thin carrot strips.
4. At one end place a handful of crisp radishes; at the other end an array of cauliflower clusters.
5. Garnish edges of tray with watercress, parsley, or other greens.
6. Side dishes of various dressings may be placed around the tray for individual selection by the guests.

STAR SALAD TRAY

Sliced tomatoes
Cucumber strips
Turnip slices
Ripe, green olives
Romaine leaves
Green onions or avocado
Thin celery strips
Thin carrot strips
Radishes
Various dressings

Amounts will vary, depending upon the number of guests.

1. On a large, round tray, arrange romaine leaves with the stem end in the center and leaves flaring out like a sunburst.
2. Place radishes in the center with the olives encircling them.
3. Place a row of tomatoes from the center to the edge of tray.
4. A third of the way around tray place a row of turnip slices, like the spokes of a wheel or the points of a star.
5. Place cucumber strips in a row to form the third spoke.
6. Next, place a row of carrot strips between the cucumber and turnip row.
7. Place the onions between the tomato slices and turnips, and the row of celery strips between the cucumber and tomato slices.
8. Serve with side dishes of various dressings for the guests to choose from.

FRUIT SALADS AROUND THE UNITED STATES

It wasn't long ago when the summer season was the only salad-time that people knew because of the scarcity of fresh fruits and vegetables during other seasons. But now that luscious, garden-fresh produce is available all year round, salad-time is any time.

Some salad combinations are so well-rounded and satisfying that they serve as a complete meal. Additionally, almost any meal can be made more dramatic and appetizing by arranging a few colorful fruits in artistic combinations and topping them with piquant dressings. Even the way the cantaloupe is zig-zagged in half or the way the pineapple is cut will add charm to table arrangements.

This section provides an assortment of fruit salads from all over the United States.

CALIFORNIA

CALIFORNIA SALAD— Variation I

SERVES 4

1 large ripe avocado
2 cups greens (romaine, endive, parsley, watercress)
½ cup cooked string beans
½ cup chopped celery
½ cup pineapple or sweet grapefruit chunks
½ cup fresh young peas
Lemon and Honey Dressing (page 78)

1. Combine greens, vegetables, and pineapple (or grapefruit) in salad bowl.
2. Cut avocado in half lengthwise. Peel and cube one half. Cut other half into strips.
3. Add the cubes to salad and toss lightly with Lemon and Honey Dressing.
4. Arrange strips on top of salad in a sunburst design.

SERVES 4

CALIFORNIA SALAD—
Variation II

Salad greens (enough to line a large salad bowl)
2 choice avocados, sliced
1 cubed mango
3 sliced bananas
1 sectioned grapefruit
1 cup pineapple chunks
1 cup watermelon balls
1 cup honeydew melon balls
Mint leaves and red cherries (as garnish)

1. Line salad bowl with salad greens.
2. Combine fruits together in bowl, tossing lightly.
3. Garnish with cherries and mint leaves. This salad requires no dressing.

SERVES 2

FRUIT SUNBURST

1 avocado, sliced
10 sweet pink grapefruit slices
Salad greens (enough to line serving tray)
10 strawberries

1. Line serving tray with salad greens.
2. Arrange slices of avocado and sweet pink grapefruit on tray.
3. Encircle with strawberries.

PERSIMMON SALAD

SERVES 4

1 head romaine
2 ripe persimmons
1 Tbs. thick sour cream
French Dressing (page 71)
1/4 cup soaked, skinned almonds

1. Arrange romaine on four salad plates.
2. Cut persimmons in half and place half on each plate.
3. Mix French Dressing with sour cream and drip over persimmons.
4. Garnish with almonds.

PEAR-DATE SALAD

SERVES 4

1 head romaine
4 pears
8 dates
2 figs
1/4 cup fresh grated coconut
1/2 cup soaked, chopped pecans
3/4 cup fresh whipped cream (mixed with honey to taste)

1. Arrange romaine on four salad plates.
2. Lay two pear halves over lettuce on each plate. Be sure to clean out seeds to create a medium-sized opening.
3. Using kitchen scissors, cut up dates and figs.
4. Combine with coconut and pecans, and place inside pear openings.
5. Add a dollop of whipped cream (with honey) to pear halves.

SERVES 4

APRICOT AND COMBINATION SALAD

1 head endive
4 ripe apricots
4 ripe nectarines
12 pitted cherries (3 on each plate)
¼ cup chopped, soaked nuts
½ cup mayonnaise (pages 73–74)

1. Wash and pit fruit and arrange on four nests of endive.
2. Combine nuts with the mayonnaise, swirling a spoonful onto each salad.

SERVES 4

AVOCADO AND APPLE SALAD

2 avocados
4 apples
½ cup grapefruit juice
Watercress sprigs (enough to line 4 salad plates)
Dressing of lemon and honey (to taste)
1 cup soaked almonds

1. Slice avocados and apples, and cover with grapefruit juice.
2. Drain before serving.
3. Place on four plates lined with watercress.
4. Sprinkle with lemon and honey, and garnish with almonds.

RAINBOW SALAD

SERVES 4

1 head shredded romaine
4 pineapple rings
8 ripe, purple plums
2 sliced bananas
1 cup strawberries
2 apricots, halved
¼ cup coconut

1. Arrange romaine leaves on four salad plates.
2. Arrange a pineapple ring on each plate of lettuce, with two plums.
3. Do the same with the banana slices and strawberries.
4. Place an apricot half on each pineapple ring.
5. Top with coconut and serve.

TROPICAL SALAD

SERVES 4

2 sliced bananas
1 16-oz. can pineapple (crushed)
½ cup chopped dates
1 16-oz. can sliced apricots
½ cup fresh seedless grapes, halved
¼ cup fresh grated coconut
2 sliced apples
1 cup whipped cream (mixed with honey to taste)

1. Combine cut fruits together in a large glass salad bowl.
2. Top with whipped cream (with honey).

SERVES 4

QUICK FRUIT PLATE—
Variation I

Salad greens (enough to line serving tray)
2 sliced avocados
3 sliced oranges
2 grapefruits, cut
1 cup whole, seedless grapes (loose)
3 sliced apples
Choice of dressing (optional)

1. Arrange salad greens on serving tray.
2. Add slices of avocado and alternate sections of orange and grapefruit.
3. Add grapes and sliced apples.
4. If desired, drizzle a dressing of your choice over the salad.

SERVES 4

QUICK FRUIT PLATE—
Variation II

Mock Cranberry Sauce (page 31)
3 sliced oranges
1 16-oz. can pineapple rings
1 cup cottage cheese
Watercress (as garnish)

1. Arrange slices of Mock Cranberry Sauce on serving tray, alternating with orange slices and pineapple rings.
2. Place a mound of cottage cheese in the center, and garnish with watercress.

MOCK CRANBERRY SAUCE   SERVES 4

1 envelope plain gelatin
1 cup boiling water
½ juiced lemon
1 cup raspberries
1–1½ cups chopped apples (depending on size of apples)

1. Blend gelatin in boiling water for half a minute, adding lemon juice gradually.
2. Add raspberries to this mixture.
3. Add apples.
4. Liquefy for three minutes and pour into mold. Chill.

FLORIDA

MANGO SALAD   SERVES 4

1 small honeyball melon
2 ripe mangoes, sliced
1–2 oranges, peeled and sliced thin
Orange Dressing (page 78)
Mint leaves

1. Pare melon and slice crosswise into four rings. Place on four salad plates.
2. Fill each ring with mango and orange slices.
3. Sprinkle with Orange Dressing and garnish with mint leaves.

SERVES 4

PAPAYA SALAD

Mint leaves
2 ripe papayas
Juice of 1 lime
½ tsp. old-fashioned brown sugar
½ cup cold-pressed salad oil

1. Arrange mint leaves on four salad plates. Cut papayas length-wise and scoop out pulp with ball scoop.
2. Heap papaya balls on nests of mint.
3. Add dressing of lime juice, oil, and brown sugar and serve immediately.

GEORGIA

SERVES 4

PLANTATION FRUIT SALAD

1 medium-sized pineapple
1 cup fresh or canned (unsweetened) apricots, sliced
1 cup sliced strawberries
1 cup fresh whipped cream
2 Tbs. honey
½ tsp. pure vanilla extract

1. Quarter pineapple lengthwise, leaving part of the leaf spray on each section. Cut out hard core and discard. Cut out pineapple from rind and slice, then cube.
2. Add the apricots and strawberries and heap into the four pine-apple shells.
3. Blend honey, vanilla, and whipped cream together and place on top.

HAWAII

FRUIT SALAD IN PINEAPPLE SHELL

SERVES 4

1 pineapple, cut into halves
2 cups papaya cubes
1 cup orange sections
1 cup banana slices
½ cup coconut milk
¾ cup fresh grated coconut

1. Scoop out pineapple halves, leaving green stem on for decorative serving.
2. Cut flesh of pineapple into cubes, and mix with other fruit. Place fruit in pineapple shells.
3. Pour coconut milk over fruit.
4. Sprinkle with fresh grated coconut.

Some Fruit Lunches

There are many fruit combinations that can make a quick, easy, and satisfying lunch. These may be varied to suit individual taste and the season. Following are a few suggestions.

- Lay strips of avocado, fan-shaped, on a serving plate. Arrange chunks of sweet oranges in the center and place small handfuls of plumped raisins in between the avocado slices. No dressing is required.

- Arrange chunks of watermelon, slices of fresh peaches, and a bunch of blue grapes on a serving plate. Deviled eggs laid on a bed of lettuce may be placed in the center.

- Pineapple and orange slices arranged with apricots around a mound of cottage cheese make a delicious as well as nutritious meal.

LOUISIANA

SERVES 4-6

FESTIVE SALAD TRAY

1 pint each of lime and orange sherbet
1 yellow melon
1 large can sliced (unsweetened) pineapple
2 cups strawberries
2 bananas, sliced diagonally
¼ watermelon, cut into chunks
2 cups light and dark grapes
Mint leaves (as garnish)

1. Place elevated glass dish in center of large serving tray and fill with round scoops of orange and lime sherbet, mingling colors.
2. Peel and slice melon in half-moons and place around rim of tray.
3. Lay slices of pineapple in the curve of each melon slice.
4. Heap strawberries and slices of banana inside the melon and pineapple ring, at one end of the tray.
5. Heap chunks of watermelon at the other end of tray.
6. Arrange grapes around base of the center sherbet dish and in all other spaces.
7. Garnish with mint leaves.

*"Health is not everything,
but without health, everything is nothing."*

Fruit Salad in Pineapple Shell.

''Nature cures, but she needs an opportunity.''

Nature's Bounty of Fresh Fruits.

FALL HOLIDAY TREAT

SERVES 4-6

Salad greens (enough to line large serving tray)
12 pear halves (with seeds scooped out)
3 pkgs. (3 oz. each) cream cheese
¹/₂ cup cherries (canned)
4 sliced peaches
Mock Cranberry-Orange Relish (page 36)
¹/₂ cup stuffed dates
¹/₂ cup pecans
4 pineapple slices
6 whole apricots
³/₄ cup blue grapes, chilled

1. Line a large tray with crisp greens.
2. Allow cream cheese to soften. Put cream cheese squares into a pastry bag. Use any tip desired.
3. At one end arrange pear halves filled with swirls of cream cheese and topped with cherries, and at other end place slices of peaches filled with Mock Cranberry–Orange Relish.
4. Place a stemmed dish in center of the tray filled with stuffed dates and pecans.
5. Arrange pineapple slices and whole apricots around it.
6. Fill in rest of space with grapes.

SERVES 4-6

MOCK CRANBERRY-ORANGE RELISH

1 envelope plain gelatin
1 cup raspberries
1 cup orange wedges
2 apples, chopped
Juice of ½ lemon
½ cup boiling water

1. Combine gelatin and boiling water, stirring for 30 seconds.
2. Slowly stir in lemon juice.
3. Add raspberries and orange sections (orange wedges should be about the same size as the raspberries).
4. Stir in chopped apples.
5. Liquefy in a blender for 3 minutes.
6. Pour into a mold and chill until firm.

Fruit Salad Tray for a Patio Party

Select a large, ripe pineapple. Cut it lengthwise into quarters, leaving a spray of leaves on each section. Cut out and discard the hard core. Carefully separate the fruit from the shell by slicing parallel to the shell. Then cut downwards to create slices, leaving the fruit in the shell.

Place these sections on a large serving tray with the leaf spray end pointing to the corners of the tray, so that the arrangement resembles the spokes of a wheel. This will leave four compartments between the "spokes."

In one compartment, place slices of ripe mango on a bed of lettuce. In the next compartment, arrange diagonal strips of banana, which have been dipped in sweetened lemon juice and rolled in coconut. In the third compartment, place strips of papaya. Finally, in the fourth compartment, heap chunks of fresh coconut.

No dressing is required for this tropical delight. If desired, though, bowls of Orange Dressing and other fruit salad dressings may be placed around the tray.

NEW ENGLAND

PRUNE AND COTTAGE CHEESE SALAD

SERVES 4

16 prunes
1/2 pound cottage cheese
Salad greens (enough to line four salad plates)
4 peach halves
1/2 cup mayonnaise (pages 73–74)
Paprika (to taste)
1/4 cup chopped nuts

1. Soak and plump prunes. Remove pits.
2. Season cottage cheese to taste and fill prunes.
3. Arrange greens on four salad plates.
4. Place a peach half in center of each plate, with four prunes around each peach.
5. Fill each peach with mayonnaise, and sprinkle with paprika and chopped nuts.

NEW YORK

SERVES 4

WALDORF SALAD

¼ cup lemon juice
½ cup water
½ cup grapes or raisins
2 cups diced apples
½ cup broken walnut meats
1 cup chopped celery
½ cup mayonnaise (pages 73–74) or whipped cream
Salad greens (enough to line large salad bowl)

1. Combine lemon juice and water in a bowl. Add apples to this mixture while being cut, to keep them from turning brown.
2. Drain apples. Do not rinse.
3. Combine apples, walnuts, celery, and grapes or raisins with mayonnaise or whipped cream.
4. Heap onto a nest of salad greens. Serve.

TEXAS

HEARTY FRUIT SALAD

SERVES 4

1 ripe pineapple, cubed
1 cup sliced strawberries
12 ripe plums, quartered
2 sweet oranges, sliced
2 fresh pears, cubed
2 sliced peaches
Honey and whipped cream or plain yogurt

1. Mix fruits together in a large salad bowl.
2. Top with honey and whipped cream mixture or yogurt. Serve.

WASHINGTON

AUTUMN SALAD

SERVES 4

3 Delicious apples
1 large, ripe banana
2 tsp. lemon juice
10 chopped dates
½ cup soaked raisins
½ cup broken pecans
1 sweet juiced orange
½ cup mayonnaise (pages 73–74)
Seeded red grapes (as garnish)

1. Slice apples and banana, place in large serving bowl, and sprinkle with lemon juice.
2. Add dates, raisins, and pecans.
3. Blend the orange juice with mayonnaise and pour over fruit.
4. Garnish with seeded red grapes.

SALADS FROM AROUND THE WORLD

As you've probably already guessed, I'm a recipe collector. In my travels to more than fifty-five countries around the world, I've eaten dozens of salads whose names I couldn't even pronounce, but whenever I found an intriguing taste or an especially nutritious combination of ingredients, I always found a way to get the recipe. I have found that those foods which enhance health also promote longevity, so whenever I've had the opportunity, I've questioned the oldest people in the areas I've visited. "What do you eat," I'd ask, "that keeps you so healthy?" Nine times out of ten, salads were among the foods they named. My list of friends includes an international roster of chefs, or so it seems.

You, too, can go around the world through your taste and appreciation of international salads—without even leaving your own kitchen. If you'd like to try your hand at some of these recipes, read on.

ARABIA

SERVES 2-4

FATTOUSH
(Mixed Salad)

3 cubed tomatoes
2 diced cucumbers
1 chopped green pepper
8 scallions, sliced thin
4 Tbs. chopped parsley
4 sprigs of fresh mint, chopped, or 1 Tbs. dried mint
½ cup olive oil
½ cup lemon juice
1 tsp. vegetable seasoning

1. Combine the tomatoes, cucumbers, green peppers, scallions, parsley, and mint in a salad bowl.
2. In another bowl, mix the oil, lemon juice, and vegetable seasoning together. Pour over vegetables.
3. Chill for one hour.

MUNKACZINA

SERVES 2-4

(Orange and Onion Salad)

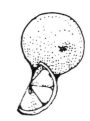

Salad greens (enough to line a serving tray)
4 oranges, sliced
3 onions, sliced
½ cup olive oil
1 tsp. vegetable seasoning
Paprika (to taste)
¼ cup small black olives, sliced

1. On a serving tray, alternate slices of orange with slices of onions on a bed of salad greens.
2. In a bowl, prepare a dressing of oil, vegetable seasoning, paprika, and olives.
3. Pour mixture over orange and onion slices.

AUSTRIA

OSTERREICHISCHER SALAT

SERVES 6

(Austrian Salad)

2 cups cubed, cooked potatoes
2 cups cubed, unpeeled raw apples
2 oz. cold-pressed, unheated vegetable oil
2 oz. natural cider vinegar
1 Tbs. vegetable broth powder
Slices of hard boiled egg (as garnish)

1. Mix potatoes and apples together.
2. Create a dressing from vegetable oil, apple cider vinegar, and vegetable broth powder (for seasoning). Pour over potatoes and apples.
3. Garnish with slices of hard boiled egg.

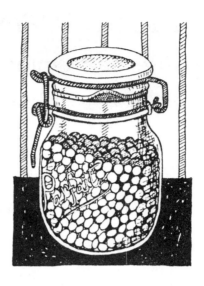

SERVES 2–4

LINSEN SALAT
(Lentil Salad)

1 cup lentils
1 onion stuck with 2 cloves
½ bay leaf
3 cups water
2 tsp. vegetable seasoning
2½ Tbs. sesame oil
1½ Tbs. natural cider vinegar
1 medium-sized onion, minced
2 Tbs. minced parsley
Quartered tomatoes (as garnish)

1. Place lentils, onion, and bay leaf in a saucepan.
2. Add water and vegetable seasoning, and simmer until lentils are tender (about 30 to 40 minutes).
3. Drain and discard bay leaf and onion.
4. Add oil, vinegar, and the minced onion. Let cool to room temperature.
5. At serving time, add parsley and mix lightly. Garnish with tomatoes.

BRAZIL

SALADA DE ABACATE

SERVES 6

(Avocado Salad)

1 clove garlic, minced
2 Tbs. grated onion
1 Tbs. chopped parsley
1 tsp. chopped chives
½ tsp. raw sugar
½ cup olive oil
2 Tbs. natural cider vinegar
1 tsp. tarragon
1 tsp. vegetable seasoning
2 heads romaine
1 head endive
1 avocado, peeled and sliced thin

1. Combine the garlic, onion, parsley, chives, sugar, olive oil, vinegar, tarragon, and vegetable seasoning in a salad bowl.
2. Mix well.
3. Tear washed and chilled romaine into pieces and add to dressing.
4. Separate endive.
5. Add avocado to endive.
6. Toss lightly with rest of salad.

BULGARIA

SERVES 4

MESHANA SALATA
(Mixed Salad with Roast Peppers)

4 green peppers
3 sliced tomatoes
2 sliced onions
2 sliced cucumbers
3 Tbs. natural cider vinegar
1/2 cup olive oil
2 tsp. vegetable seasoning

1. Wash and dry peppers. Then one at a time, place each on a fork, and hold over a flame until the skins turn brown. Peel off the skin and cut each pepper into one-inch strips. Chill for one hour.
2. Combine the peppers, tomatoes, onions, and cucumbers in a large salad bowl.
3. Mix vinegar, oil, and vegetable seasoning together in another bowl. Pour over salad.
4. Toss carefully and chill before serving.

CHILE

SERVES 4

ENSALADA CAMPESINA
(Peasant Salad)

1 cup dried chick peas or 2 cups canned, drained garbanzos
1/2 lb. diced cream cheese
2 onions, sliced thin
1/2 cup olive oil
1/4 cup lemon juice
1 tsp. vegetable seasoning
1/2 tsp. ground coriander
3 hard boiled eggs, chopped (as garnish)
Salad greens (enough to line a serving tray)

1. Soak the chick peas (or garbanzos) in water overnight. Drain well.
2. Add fresh water and cook for two hours or until tender. Drain well and chill for two hours.
3. Combine the chick peas, onions, and cream cheese in a bowl.
4. Mix the olive oil, lemon juice, vegetable seasoning, and coriander together in another bowl. Pour over chick pea mixture and toss lightly.
5. Place on lettuce-lined tray and garnish with eggs.

COLOMBIA

PICANTE DE HUEVOS   SERVES 4
(Egg and Avocado Salad)

6 hard boiled eggs, chopped
2 avocados, chopped fine
1 fresh chili pepper, chopped fine (or 1/4 tsp. of dried chili pepper)
1 onion, chopped fine
3 Tbs. chopped parsley
2 Tbs. natural cider vinegar
1 1/2 tsp. vegetable seasoning
Lettuce (enough to line a serving tray)

1. Combine all ingredients together in a large bowl.
2. Mix well until all are blended together. Chill.
3. Serve on a bed of lettuce.

DENMARK

SERVES 6

RODKAAL SALAT
(Red Cabbage Salad)

1 red cabbage
1 large apple
1 celery heart
1 cup heavy cream
1 juiced lemon
1 tsp. vegetable seasoning
1 Tbs. raw sugar

1. Wash and drain cabbage, then grate it.
2. Cut apple up into small pieces.
3. Chop celery into fine pieces.
4. Whip the cream, adding lemon juice, vegetable seasoning, and sugar (honey may be substituted for the sugar). Add this creamy dressing in a large bowl to the cabbage, apple, and celery.

SERVES 2

AGURKESALAT
(Cucumber Salad)

³/4 cup sour cream
1 tsp. chopped green onion
1 tsp. vegetable seasoning
2 Tbs. natural cider vinegar
2 medium-sized cucumbers (pared if skins are bitter), sliced
Leaf lettuce or other greens (for lining serving plate)
Paprika (as garnish)

1. Mix the sour cream, onion, vegetable seasoning, and vinegar together in a bowl.
2. Add the cucumbers and toss lightly.
3. Serve on lettuce leaves and garnish with paprika.

EGYPT

FOOL MUDAMMAS

SERVES 2-4

(Beans, Egyptian Style)

1¹/₂ cups white beans
2 tsp. vegetable seasoning
2 cloves garlic
¹/₂ cup olive oil
¹/₄ cup lemon juice
3 scallions, sliced fine
1 head romaine

1. Wash the beans thoroughly and soak overnight in water. Cook beans until the skins split (about two hours). Drain well and cool.
2. Place beans in a bowl; add vegetable seasoning, garlic, olive oil, and lemon juice, and mix well. Chill.
3. Serve on a bed of romaine, tossed with finely-sliced scallions.

ENGLAND

NEW LEEK SALAD

SERVES 4

3 leeks
1 large tomato
1 head romaine
1 tsp. sweet basil
1 tsp. chervil
Garlic (for seasoning bowl)
¹/₂ cup olive oil
2 tsp. vegetable seasoning
2 Tbs. natural cider vinegar

1. Rub a large wooden bowl with garlic.
2. Coarsely cut up the white part of the leeks. Place in garlic-seasoned bowl.
3. Cut large tomato into sections. Add tomato and romaine lettuce to bowl.
4. Sprinkle with sweet basil and chervil.
5. Dress with olive oil, vegetable seasoning, and vinegar.

YORKSHIRE SALAD

SERVES 6

3 Tbs. cold-pressed olive oil
3 Tbs. molasses
6 Tbs. natural cider vinegar
2 heads lettuce, shredded
3 scallions, sliced fine

1. Combine the first three ingredients in a blender. Liquefy for 1 minute.
2. Toss scallions and shredded lettuce in a separate bowl.
3. Dress with blenderized olive oil, molasses, and vinegar.

FRANCE

SALADE DE PISSENLIT

(Dandelion Salad)

SERVES 2

4 cups young dandelion leaves
2 Tbs. olive oil
1 Tbs. natural cider vinegar
Vegetable seasoning (to taste)

1. Place dandelion leaves in a large glass salad bowl.
2. Dress with olive oil, vinegar, and vegetable seasoning.

SALADE DE LAITUES A LA CREME

SERVES 4

(Lettuce Salad with Cream)

1 head lettuce
2 hard boiled eggs
4-6 Tbs. heavy cream
Vegetable seasoning (to taste)
Honey (to taste)
2 Tbs. lemon juice

1. Shred lettuce and place in a large glass salad bowl.
2. Pound the yolks of hard boiled eggs in a mortar. When reduced to a paste, place in a second bowl.
3. Add heavy cream, gradually working it with a wooden spoon until it is the consistency of thin mayonnaise.
4. Season with vegetable seasoning and honey. Add lemon juice very gradually, stirring continuously.
5. Pour over lettuce. Serve.

GERMANY

SERVES 2

SALAT VON ROTE RUBEN

2 cups thinly-sliced, cooked beets
½ cup sliced radishes
¼ cup chopped shallots
Natural cider vinegar (to taste)
Vegetable seasoning (to taste)
Raw sugar or honey (to taste)
Caraway seed (to taste)
1 chopped bay leaf
Beet juice (to taste)

1. Combine beets, radishes, and shallots together in a large mixing bowl.
2. Dress with vinegar, vegetable seasoning, raw sugar or honey, caraway seed, chopped bay leaf, and beet juice.

KALTER KARTOFFELSALAT   SERVES 4
(Cold Potato Salad)

1 lb. potatoes, boiled in skins
1 tsp. raw sugar
1/2 tsp. vegetable seasoning
1/2 tsp. dry mustard
2 Tbs. natural cider vinegar
1 cup sour cream
1/2 cup thinly-sliced cucumbers
Paprika (to taste)

1. Slice potatoes while still warm. (If new potatoes, slice in their jackets; if old, they should be peeled.)
2. Mix sugar, vegetable seasoning, mustard, and vinegar together in a bowl.
3. Add sour cream and cucumbers, and mix lightly with the potatoes.
4. Turn into a serving dish and sprinkle with paprika. Serve warm or cool.

GREECE

SERVES 4

SALATA
(Salad)

1 small head white cabbage
2 beets
1 cup small black olives
4 Tbs. olive oil
3 Tbs. natural cider vinegar
1 tsp. dry mustard
Vegetable seasoning (to taste)

1. Shred cabbage and beets.
2. Toss with small black olives.
3. Dress with olive oil, natural cider vinegar, dry mustard, and vegetable seasoning.
4. Mix well and serve.

INDONESIA

GADO-GADO

SERVES 4–6

(Vegetable Salad)

2 Tbs. olive oil
¼ cup finely-chopped onions
2 minced garlic cloves
½ cup peanut butter
1 tsp. raw sugar or honey
½ tsp. sea salt
2 Tbs. grated lemon rind
¾ cup coconut milk or light cream
1 cup cooked, sliced green beans
1 cup shredded cabbage, steamed for 5 minutes
2 cups diced tomatoes
2 cups sliced cucumbers
2 cups hard boiled eggs, chopped coarsely
Shredded greens or lettuce (for lining serving plate)

1. Heat oil in skillet. Sauté onions and garlic for three minutes.
2. Stir in peanut butter, sugar or honey, salt, and lemon rind. Gradually add the coconut milk (or light cream) mixed with water.
3. Cook over low heat for five minutes, stirring frequently. Cool.
4. Make a bed of shredded greens and arrange the beans, cabbage, tomatoes, and cucumbers over it.
5. Sprinkle with chopped eggs.
6. Serve the dressing in a separate bowl.

ITALY

SERVES 2

ITALIAN PEPPER SALAD

2 large green peppers
4 Tbs. salad oil
1 Tbs. natural cider vinegar
Vegetable seasoning (to taste)

1. Char the peppers on the outside by placing each on a fork, one at a time, and holding it over a flame until it is black all over. Cool under running water and rub off outer charred membrane.
2. Halve the peppers, removing and discarding the seeds. Slice into thin lengths and add oil, vinegar, and vegetable seasoning.
3. Let stand half an hour to marinate before serving.

SERVES 4

INSALATA DI FINOCCHIO, POMODORA E CICORI

(Fennel, Tomato, and Chicory Salad)

1 head finocchio (fennel)
2 large, firm tomatoes
1 small head chicory
8-10 leaves of fresh, sweet basil
6 Tbs. olive oil
1 clove garlic
2 Tbs. natural cider vinegar
Vegetable seasoning (to taste)

1. Wash greens and tomatoes and drain.
2. Cut finocchio into thin slices.
3. Break chicory into 2-inch pieces.
4. Quarter tomatoes.
5. Rub bowl with garlic, adding basil, greens, and vegetables.
6. Blend oil, vinegar, and vegetable seasoning together and add to salad. Toss thoroughly, and serve.

Snacks to Serve With Salads

Bread Sticks

Cut whole grain bread into thin strips, sprinkle with grated cheese, and toast under grill. Serve hot.

Cheese Sticks

Cut graham bread into slices. Spread with butter and grated cheese, and make into sandwiches. Toast and serve.

Corn Fingers

Bake corn bread in lady finger molds. Serve either hot or cold with a salad of your choice.

Fruit Bread

Cut date nut bread or another healthy loaf of your own choosing into squares. Spread with prune-orange paste or whatever tasty spread you desire and serve with a salad.

Nut Bread Rounds

Slice a round loaf of nut bread. Spread with chopped olive and cream cheese spread. Serve at once or refrigerate until later.

Sandwiches

All sandwiches made with whole grain bread are delicious served with salads, and make a hearty meal when served with the right combinations.

Different kinds of whole grain health breads may be cut into triangles, circles, squares, diamonds, or half-moons and spread with fillings of nut, cheese, dried fruit, or olives. Fancy crackers can also be spread with suitable dips, spreads, or sandwich fillings. Those made with aged cheese or egg mixtures may be toasted and served hot along with hot spiced apple juice on cool evenings or as winter snacks.

Fruit Tempters

On a large platter, arrange the following fruits:

* pitted dates stuffed with cream cheese or nuts
* banana sections rolled in macaroon coconut
* peeled tangerines, with the segments separated and opened like a flower
* stuffed olives
* melon balls rolled in fine coconut
* berries or apricot halves garnished with sprigs of mint
* pineapple sections sprinkled with chopped nuts
* pitted prunes stuffed with a filling of raw nut butter and cherry concentrate
* scalloped lemon baskets filled with nuts
* slices of fresh coconut

All of the above need not be used on the same tray at the same time—they are merely suggestions. Others may be substituted to suit the individual tastes of your guests.

JAMAICA

SERVES 4-6

IRIS SALAD

3 tomatoes, peeled and sliced ½-inch thick
2 bananas, diced
3 hard cooked eggs, sliced
¼ cup chopped, blanched almonds
2 heads romaine
1 Tbs. chopped green olives
1 Tbs. chopped green pepper
1 clove minced garlic
½ cup natural cider vinegar
½ tsp. vegetable seasoning
¼ tsp. paprika
¾ cup olive oil
1 Tbs. chopped pimento
1 dash salt

1. Place garlic in vinegar for thirty minutes, then discard garlic.
2. Combine salt, paprika, oil, vegetable seasoning, and vinegar in a bowl and mix all ingredients thoroughly.
3. Add the green pepper, pimento, and olives and mix well.
4. Arrange torn pieces of romaine on plates.
5. Place two slices of tomato on each plate of romaine.
6. Add slices of egg, diced bananas, and almonds.
7. Pour dressing over each plate.

KOREA

KOOUG NAMUL KOREAN

SERVES 4

(Bean Sprout Salad)

1 cup fresh bean sprouts
1½ Tbs. finely-chopped green onions, (including tops)
1 Tbs. sesame or salad oil
1 Tbs. browned and pulverized sesame seeds
3 Tbs. soy sauce
⅛ tsp. chopped garlic
Vegetable seasoning (to taste)

1. Steam the bean sprouts for a few minutes. (If canned bean sprouts are used, simply drain; steaming is unnecessary.) Add vegetable seasoning, onions, oil, sesame seeds, soy sauce, and garlic.
2. Mix well.
3. Chill and serve cooled.

SOOK CHOO NA MOOL

SERVES 4

(Bean Sprout Salad)

¼ cup sesame oil
2 Tbs. natural cider vinegar
2 Tbs. soy sauce
½ tsp. vegetable seasoning
¼ cup finely-chopped scallions
¼ cup julienne pimento
2 Tbs. ground sesame seeds
1 minced garlic clove
2 cups bean sprouts

1. Mix oil, vinegar, soy sauce, vegetable seasoning, scallions, pimento, sesame seeds, and garlic together.
2. Pour over sprouts in a large bowl.
3. Toss and chill for one hour.

SERVES 4-6

MU SAINGCH'AI
(Turnip Salad)

3 cups sliced turnips (5 medium-sized)
2 cups sliced apples or pears
1⅓ Tbs. finely-chopped green onions (including tops)
3 Tbs. soy sauce
1 Tbs. browned and pulverized sesame seeds
4½ tsp. raw sugar or 1 Tbs. honey
1 tsp. vegetable seasoning
2½ tsp. natural cider vinegar
1½ tsp. sesame or salad oil
Red pepper strips (as garnish)

1. Combine vinegar, onions, oil, soy sauce, and sesame seeds. Toss with sliced turnips.
2. Mix in vegetable seasoning and sugar or honey.
3. Add slices of apple or pear.
4. Garnish with red pepper strips.

MEXICO

SERVES 4

GUACAMOLE
(Avocado Salad)

2 avocados
1 small onion or 3 green onions
1 tomato, peeled
1 tsp. vegetable seasoning
Juice of 1 lemon
Lettuce (enough to line serving tray)

1. Chop onion and tomato very fine.
2. In a separate bowl, mash the avocados with a wooden spoon.
3. Add avocados to onion and tomato mixture.
4. Add vegetable seasoning and lemon juice.
5. Serve on a bed of lettuce leaves.

NORWAY

SELLERI OG EPLE SALAT

SERVES 4

(Celery and Apple Salad)

1½ cups chopped celery
2 large apples
1 hard boiled egg (separate white from yolk)
1 Tbs. safflower oil
1 Tbs. fresh cream
2 tsp. natural cider vinegar
¼ tsp. vegetable seasoning
1 tsp. raw sugar or honey
1 head lettuce
Paprika (to taste)

1. Steam chopped celery until slightly soft. Chill.
2. Cut apples into small cubes. Combine with celery.
3. Mash egg yolk smooth with oil. Add cream, vinegar, vegetable seasoning, and sugar or honey.
4. Beat well and pour over apples and celery.
5. Toss on top of lettuce, garnish with egg whites (chopped fine) and paprika.

PAKISTAN

MASTE KHIAR

SERVES 4-6

(Cucumbers with Yogurt)

4 cucumbers
¼ cup chopped mint
3 8-oz. containers plain yogurt
Vegetable seasoning (to taste)

1. Cut cucumbers into small cubes.
2. Add the mint and two containers of yogurt and vegetable seasoning.
3. Mix and chill for two hours.
4. Drain off excess water and add the remaining container of yogurt.

RUSSIA

SERVES 6-8

ROUSSKI SALAT
(Russian Salad)

2 sliced cucumbers
4-6 potatoes, cooked in skins and cubed
3 beets, cooked and cubed
2 cups sauerkraut
2 cups kidney beans
4 hard boiled eggs
½ cup sliced ripe olives
Vegetable seasoning (to taste)
1 cup sesame oil
½ cup natural cider vinegar
Dry mustard (to taste)

1. Toss cucumbers, potatoes, beets, kidney beans, and sauerkraut together lightly.
2. Make a dressing of two parts oil to one part natural cider vinegar. Add vegetable seasoning and dry mustard to this mixture.
3. Pour dressing over salad.
4. Add hard boiled eggs and sliced, ripe olives. Serve cold.

VINAIGRETTE

SERVES 4–6

(Summer Salad)

8-10 new potatoes, cubed
½ lb. mushrooms, sliced and cooked
2 beets, cubed and cooked
2 cucumbers, cubed
½ cup chopped parsley
⅔ cup olive oil
⅓ cup natural cider vinegar
Vegetable seasoning (to taste)
Dry mustard (to taste)

1. Mix equal parts of cold, cubed, new potatoes (with skins); mushrooms (if small, leave whole); beets; fresh cucumber; and parsley.
2. Toss lightly with dressing made of two parts oil to one part natural cider vinegar, vegetable seasoning, and dry mustard.

SPAIN

ESCALIBADA

SERVES 2

(Cooked Pimentos and Eggplant)

2 fresh pimentos
1 eggplant
4 Tbs. olive oil
1½ Tbs. natural cider vinegar
Vegetable seasoning (to taste)

1. Cut fresh pimentos and eggplant in half and sprinkle with 1 Tbs. oil. Bake until tender.
2. When done, skin both pimentos and eggplant, chop, and dress with 3 Tbs. oil, natural cider vinegar, and vegetable seasoning.
3. Serve cold.

SERVES 2-4

GAZPACHO
(Cold Salad)

1 clove garlic
3 lbs. tomatoes
2 medium-sized cucumbers
½ cup minced green pepper
½ cup minced green onion
2 cups tomato juice
⅓ cup olive oil
3 Tbs. natural cider vinegar
2 tsp. paprika
Vegetable seasoning (to taste)
Dash of salt

1. Rub a large bowl with cut garlic clove. (Discard garlic clove.)
2. Peel tomatoes, remove seeds, and chop into small pieces. Be sure not to lose any of their juice; pour the tomatoes along with juice into garlic-rubbed bowl.
3. If cucumbers are bitter, peel; otherwise, chop up cucumbers, including peel. Combine with the onion and green pepper. Add to the chopped tomatoes.
4. Next add the tomato juice.
5. Combine the olive oil, natural cider vinegar, salt, and paprika, and add to the other vegetables.
6. Season with vegetable seasoning.
7. Chill thoroughly before serving.

SWEDEN

RODBETSALLAD
SERVES 4–6

(Cabbage and Beet Salad)

1 head lettuce
2 cups shredded cabbage
2 cups grated carrots
2 cups grated raw beets
French Dressing (see recipe below)
Russian Dressing (see recipe below)

1. Chill vegetables in refrigerator.
2. Sprinkle the shredded cabbage with French Dressing and toss well.
3. Arrange the vegetables separately on lettuce, alternating colors.
4. Place a bowl of Russian dressing in center to be served on top.

French Dressing is made by combining 4 Tbs. oil and 2 Tbs. natural cider vinegar, with vegetable seasoning to taste.

Russian Dressing is made by combining 1½ cups mayonnaise, ½ cup cream, 1 Tbs. grated horseradish, and ½ cup chili sauce. (See recipe below.) Mix well and chill.

Chili Sauce
¼ cup tomato juice
2 cups sliced tomatoes
⅜ cup natural cider vinegar
¼ cup diced green pepper
½ cup sliced onions
¼ cup old-fashioned brown sugar
3 tsp. vegetable seasoning
¼ tsp. celery salt
¼ tsp. dry mustard
¼ tsp. chili powder

1. Blend first three ingredients in a liquefier until smooth.
2. Add and blend the remainder of ingredients until vegetables are chopped (about two seconds).

SWITZERLAND

SERVES 2

RAW MUESLI

2 apples (cut into quarters)
½ orange, peeled
½ lemon, peeled
1 cup milk
2 Tbs. honey
½ cup oat flakes
Heavy cream

1. Place apples, orange, and lemon in a blender with the milk and honey. Mix for twenty seconds.
2. Put oat flakes in a plate or bowl and pour in ingredients from blender.
3. Mix well. Serve with heavy cream.

SERVES 2

MUESLI WITH BERRIES

3 Tbs. soaked hazel nuts
1 cup plain yogurt
1 cup cottage cheese
4 Tbs. raw sugar
2 cups raspberries or strawberries
½ cup oat flakes
Heavy cream

1. Combine first five ingredients in a blender for twenty seconds.
2. Put oat flakes in a plate or bowl and pour in ingredients from blender.
3. Mix well. Serve with heavy cream.

TURKEY

JAJIK

(Cucumber Salad)

4 cucumbers
1 tsp. vegetable seasoning
1 Tbs. natural cider vinegar
1 tsp. chopped dill
2 cups plain yogurt
3 Tbs. olive oil
1 Tbs. chopped mint
1 clove garlic
Chopped greens (enough to line serving tray)

1. Slice cucumbers, and sprinkle with vegetable seasoning.
2. Soak the garlic in vinegar for ten minutes. Strain.
3. Add the dill and vinegar to the yogurt.
4. Add olive oil, and mix well.
5. Pour over cucumbers and mix well.
6. Serve on chopped greens and sprinkle with chopped mint.

URUGUAY

SALSA CRILLESA

(Carrot Salad)

3 large carrots
3 medium-sized onions
3 bay leaves
1/4 tsp. oregano
1/2 cup natural cider vinegar
1/2 cup olive oil
Vegetable seasoning (to taste)

1. Chop carrots and onions very fine.
2. Steam with bay leaves and oregano.
3. Add oil, vinegar, and vegetable seasoning.
4. Cool before serving.

VENEZUELA

SERVES 4

ENSALADA DE ESPINACA Y AGUACATE
(Avocado Spinach Salad)

½ lb. spinach
2 Tbs. olive oil
2 sliced onions
½ tsp. vegetable seasoning
1 avocado, peeled and sliced
1 hard boiled egg
1 head lettuce
½ cup mayonnaise (pages 73–74) or sour cream

1. Steam the washed spinach for one minute.
2. Heat oil in a skillet. Add onions and vegetable seasoning. Sauté for five minutes, stirring.
3. Place onions in chopping bowl, and add spinach, avocado, and egg. Chop until mixture is well blended. Chill for one hour.
4. Place lettuce leaves on plates, spooning avocado mixture over the lettuce.
5. Serve with mayonnaise or sour cream on top.

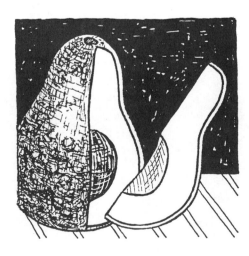

''Man shall not live by carrot juice alone!''

Party Salad With Selection of Dressings.

''It is not what we do once in a while that counts;
it's what we do most of the time.''

Salad Sprouts.

Some Tasty Beverages to Serve With Salads

Although a beverage is not necessary to make a salad meal complete, some people like to serve a healthful drink along with sandwiches and salads, as a complement. Or you may wish to serve a beverage alone, simply as a refreshment. Here are a few suggestions.

SERVES 4

Hot Spiced Apple Juice

4 cups apple juice
3 whole cloves
2 cinnamon sticks
1 tsp. fresh nutmeg

1. Bring apple juice to a boil; add whole cloves, cinnamon sticks, and fresh nutmeg.
2. Boil until flavored according to taste.
3. Serve hot or cold.

SERVES 4-6

Pineapple-Grape Punch

1 quart (32 oz.) liquid grape juice concentrate
1 16-oz. can unsweetened pineapple juice
1½ cups water

Because juice is concentrated, water should be added, particularly for children.

1. Combine grape juice concentrate with pineapple juice.
2. Add water to dilute and serve chilled.

SERVES 4

Oriental Tea Punch

4 cups water
2 mandarin orange tea bags
2 Red Zinger tea bags
1 Tbs. cherry concentrate
2 tsp. lemon juice
Sugar or honey (optional)

1. Boil water and brew tea combination.
2. Add cherry concentrate and lemon juice. If additional sweetening is desired, other fruit juices, raw sugar, or honey may be added.

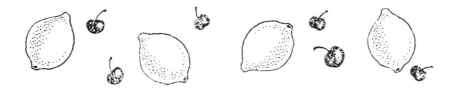

SERVES 4

Minted Lemonade

½ cup lemon juice
½ cup tupelo honey
Mint leaves (1 Tbs. chopped; 4 whole sprigs)
2 cups water

1. Combine honey with 1 cup of hot water. Add chopped mint leaves.
2. Let stand for five or ten minutes, then strain into pitcher.
3. Add lemon juice and 1 cup of water to the mint-honey mixture and pour into chilled glasses.
4. Garnish each glass with a sprig of whole mint.

3. DRESSING UP RIGHT: Basic and Best Salad Dressings

Salad dressings add a special pizzazz to salad ingredients, enhancing both their flavor and their nutritional value. The only cautions we need to observe are in watching calories and being aware of the chemical additives present in most commercial dressings. I recommend that you make your own dressings, using only the highest-quality natural oils and vinegars (see page 8).

There is no "correct" recipe for salad dressings, since slight variations in ingredients may be necessary to please particular palates. Our tastes do change from time to time, making experimenting with ingredients a worthwhile investment. What I'm providing you with in this chapter is a basic recipe and variations for several kinds of dressings. Although each one is delicious, I still encourage you to experiment to find out what you like best. Always keep in mind that a salad dressing should complement a salad nutritionally, as well as tastefully.

HERB SALAD DRESSING   MAKES 1 CUP

1 clove garlic
1 Tbs. chopped basil
1 Tbs. chopped chives
1 Tbs. chopped parsley
1 Tbs. chopped chervil
³/₄ cup olive oil
¹/₄ cup herb vinegar

1. Combine ingredients together in a jar and shake well.
2. Refrigerate overnight.

BASIC FRENCH DRESSING   MAKES 1 CUP

¹/₄ cup lemon juice
¹/₂ cup olive or salad oil
Juice of one tomato or ¹/₄ cup tomato juice
Vegetable seasoning (to taste)

1. Mix all ingredients together thoroughly.
2. Serve over salad.

OR

¹/₄ cup vinegar
¹/₂ cup cold-pressed safflower, sesame, or olive oil
Juice of one tomato or ¹/₄ cup tomato juice
Vegetable seasoning (to taste)

1. Mix all ingredients together thoroughly.
2. Serve over salad.

24 WAYS TO LOVE YOUR BASIC FRENCH DRESSING

With your basic French dressing in hand, you can create your own special blends by adding one or more of the following ingredients to the above recipe. Feel free to add as little or as much of these suggested "extras" to satisfy your own particular taste.

- Honey
- Juice of orange or lemon
- Mashed avocado
- Chopped parsley
- Chopped chives
- Chopped onion or onion juice
- Chopped celery
- Sesame seeds
- Mustard
- Horseradish
- Diced black olives
- Any herb you desire
- Sour cream
- Cottage cheese
- Roquefort cheese
- Grated Parmesan cheese
- Chopped pimentos and green peppers

- 1 Tbs. each of olives, parsley, and green peppers
- 1 pimento, chopped fine; ½ cup Roquefort cheese; 1 small onion, minced; 1 hard boiled egg, chopped fine.
- 1 cup sour cream; ½ cup tomato juice; 1 tsp. paprika
- ⅛ tsp. saffron for each cup of dressing
- 1 hard boiled egg, chopped fine; 2 Tbs. parsley; 2 tsp. chopped onion; ½ cup chopped, cooked beets
- ¼ cup blanched almonds; 1 Tbs. shredded orange peel; mint leaves; fresh dill
- 3 tomatoes, mashed; ⅛ tsp. oregano; pinch thyme; ¼ cup Parmesan cheese

BASIC MAYONNAISE WITH EGGS

MAKES 2½ CUPS

2 whole eggs
4 Tbs. lemon juice
½ tsp. vegetable seasoning
2 cups olive oil

If any mayonnaise or mayonnaise combination is left over, be sure to store under refrigeration, as it is subject to bacterial growth that cannot be seen or smelled.

1. Place first three ingredients in a blender, along with ½ cup olive oil, and turn power on high.
2. Remove cover, and continue to blend as you add a thin, steady stream of 1½ cups oil.
3. As soon as all the oil has been added, turn off power.
4. Remove from blender and serve.

BASIC MAYONNAISE WITHOUT EGGS

MAKES 2 CUPS

1 cup heavy cream
1 tsp. raw sugar
Dash of paprika
Pinch of vegetable seasoning
1 cup olive oil
2 Tbs. lemon juice

1. Chill mixing bowl and ingredients.
2. Combine dry ingredients with cream, and whip with wire whisk or electric mixer.
3. Add oil slowly while beating.
4. Add lemon juice a few drops at a time, alternating with the oil, as dressing thickens. Beat constantly as you add lemon juice and oil.

MAKES 1 CUP

BASIC MAYONNAISE WITH EGG YOLK

1 egg yolk
1/2 tsp. raw sugar
Dash of vegetable seasoning
1/4 tsp. dry mustard
3/4 cup olive oil or other salad oil
1 Tbs. lemon juice

1. Combine egg yolk and dry ingredients. Beat well with wire whisk or electric mixer.
2. Add oil a few drops at a time while beating.
3. Slowly add lemon juice while beating.

BEYOND BASIC MAYONNAISE

Mayonnaise can be used as a spread as well as a dressing. By adding some of the following ingredients to one of the basic recipes, you can vary its taste, its consistency, and its color. Feel free to use as little or as much as you like. (And don't be afraid to be a little creative!)

- Chopped cucumber and fresh mint leaves
- Chopped green pepper
- Chopped chives, chervil, and dill
- 2 Tbs. honey for each cup of mayonnaise
- Hard boiled egg, chopped fine
- Chopped watercress or parsley
- Horseradish
- Mashed banana and 1 Tbs. orange juice
- Chopped, large black olives
- Chopped pimentos and tomato purée
- Any herb you desire
- Fresh whipped cream

BASIC SOUR CREAM DRESSING

MAKES 1½ CUPS

1 cup sour cream
½ cup lemon juice

1. Mix ingredients together thoroughly.
2. This dressing tastes best when served over fruit salads, but it may be used with vegetable salads as well.

MORE THAN JUST SOUR CREAM

As with the basic recipes for French dressing and mayonnaise, sour cream dressing can also be "spiced up" by adding any one of the following, in the amounts desired.

- Honey
- Crushed pineapple and raw sugar
- Mashed avocado and minced onion
- Chopped radishes, cucumbers, and scallions
- Jerusalem artichoke, puréed
- Chopped peppermint, parsley, bean sprouts, and minced onions
- Parsley
- Minced scallions
- Tomato juice and honey

MAKES 1½ CUPS

BASIC YOGURT DRESSING

1 cup plain yogurt
½ cup lemon juice

1. Mix ingredients together thoroughly.
2. Serve over salad.

YOGURT VARIATIONS

For some delicious taste variations, you might try adding one of the following to the basic recipe, depending upon individual preference.

- 1 Tbs. Roquefort or other cheese
- Crushed pineapple and raw sugar
- Mashed avocado and minced onion
- Chopped radishes, cucumbers, and scallions
- Jerusalem artichoke, puréed
- Chopped peppermint, parsley, bean sprouts, and minced onions
- Parsley
- Minced scallions

MAKES 1½ CUPS

BASIC COTTAGE CHEESE DRESSING

1 cup cottage cheese
½ cup lemon juice

1. Mix ingredients together thoroughly.
2. Serve over salad.

COTTAGE CHEESE ADDITIONS

Using the basic recipe above as a base, try your hand at creating some delicious and taste-tingling creations of your own by adding one of the following. Use as little or as much as you like.

- Parmesan cheese, French dressing, vegetable seasoning, puréed garlic
- Fresh mint, orange juice
- Grated cheddar cheese, ½ cup cream, vegetable seasoning, 1 ripe avocado
- Yogurt or sour cream, Roquefort cheese
- Apricot nectar, ¼ cup mayonnaise, vegetable seasoning
- Paprika, vegetable seasoning, chopped olives
- Fresh cream, pineapple juice
- 2 Tbs. honey, ¼ tsp. grated lemon rind, ¼ to ½ cup olive oil, vegetable seasoning
- Sour cream, diced cucumbers, ½ cup green onions, ½ cup sliced radishes, green pepper rings

OIL AND VINEGAR DRESSING MAKES 1 CUP

¼ cup apple cider vinegar or wine vinegar
¾ cup cold-pressed safflower, sesame, or olive oil
Vegetable seasoning (to taste)
½ clove minced garlic (optional)
Pinch each of parsley, oregano, dill, sweet basil, and thyme (optional)
Twist of lemon peel (optional)

1. Combine all ingredients together and mix well. (If desired, an herbal-flavored oil and vinegar dressing can be made by adding ½ clove minced garlic and a pinch each of parsley, fresh oregano, dill, sweet basil, thyme, and a twist of lemon peel. Let steep for one to two weeks.)
2. Serve over salad greens.

MAKES 1 CUP

VINAIGRETTE DRESSING

½ cup sesame oil
¼ cup lemon juice
¼ cup tomato juice
1 Tbs. chopped olives
1 Tbs. chopped green pepper
1 Tbs. minced parsley

1. Mix liquid ingredients together well.
2. Stir in solid ingredients.
3. Serve over salad greens.

MAKES 1½ CUPS

ORANGE DRESSING

½ cup chopped olives
1 small green bell pepper, chopped
½ cup vegetable broth powder
Juice from 1 orange
¼ cup safflower oil
2 Tbs. lemon juice

1. Blend liquid ingredients together.
2. Stir in vegetable broth powder.
3. Add olives and pepper, mixing thoroughly.
4. Serve over fruit salad.

MAKES 1 CUP

LEMON AND HONEY DRESSING

⅔ cup lemon juice
⅓ cup salad oil
3 Tbs. honey

1. Blend ingredients thoroughly.
2. Serve over vegetable or fruit salad.

FRUIT DRESSING

SERVES 1

3 tsp. lemon juice
3 tsp. orange juice
4 tsp. safflower oil
1 tsp. honey

1. Pour all ingredients into a glass jar and shake well.
2. Serve over salad.

AVOCADO DRESSING

SERVES 2

1 avocado
Juice of 1 orange, lemon, or papaya

1. Beat the pulp of the avocado until it is the consistency of whipped cream.
2. Add juice very gradually to season.
3. Whip with a rotary beater until a whipped cream consistency is reached.
4. Serve over salad.

COCONUT DRESSING

MAKES ½ CUP

¹/₄ cup coconut milk
2 tsp. honey
¹/₄ cup salad oil

Ideally, coconut milk is obtained by splitting open a fresh coconut; the liquid inside is the milk. If you don't have a coconut on hand, though, you can use unsweetened canned or powdered coconut milk.

1. Mix ingredients thoroughly.
2. Serve over salad.

MAKES 2½ CUPS

HIDDEN VALLEY DELIGHT— VARIATION I

¼ cup lemon juice
3 cloves of garlic, crushed
¼ cup raw sugar
¼ tsp. herb seasoning
¼ tsp. vegetable seasoning
2 cups sour cream

1. Blend lemon juice with garlic.
2. Add remainder of ingredients and blend thoroughly.
3. Serve over salad, particularly greens and cole slaw.

MAKES 2½-2¾ CUPS

HIDDEN VALLEY DELIGHT— VARIATION II

¼ cup lemon juice
¼ tsp. nutmeg
¼-½ cup raw sugar
¼ tsp. herb seasoning
¼ tsp. vegetable seasoning
2 cups sour cream

1. Blend all ingredients together thoroughly, adding sugar to taste.
2. Serve over salad, particularly fruit salad.

4. *TASTY SOUPS:*
Nutrition in a Bowl

AN INTRODUCTION TO SOUPS

Nothing tastes better than a hot bowl of soup on a cold winter day. However, don't limit yourself to hot soups. A cold soup on a hot summer day can be quite refreshing! Hot or cold, soups are a delicious and nutritious part of any meal. When soup is part of your lunch or dinner, it's important that it harmonizes with the rest of the meal. Many of us think of soup as the introductory course to a meal—the course that whets our appetites for what is to come. Actually, a nutritious soup can be a whole meal in itself.

SOUPS FOR HEALTH

Soups should be not only tasty and attractive looking, but nutritious as well. They should help to correct deficiencies and maintain proper nutrient levels. Most important, you should be able to prepare a hearty soup without a lot of work. In less than an hour you should be able to create a nutritious soup from scratch and be ready to serve it.

I have traveled across several continents and spoken with some of the oldest men in the world. Many have offered some helpful suggestions that may be of interest to you. One soup that was mentioned very often as promoting longevity was made from cooking the jelly out of fresh veal joints. I later discovered that this broth was high in sodium. It is excellent for rheumatism, arthritis, and catarrhal elimination. It is good for the stomach, bowel, ligaments, joints, and glands. (See recipe on page 147.)

In this age of calcium problems and deficiencies, such as osteoporosis, many might be helped by following this soup recipe. The gelatin from joint material is comprised of 48 percent calcium. This soup is a good source of this essential element.

Aside from this healthful broth, soups should generally be made without meat. The vegetables and greens that your soup contains will provide the essential nutrients, such as sodium and calcium, that your body needs. If you need more sodium in your diet, you can enrich your soup by adding whey powder to the broth just before serving.

One nutritious vegetable to use in your soup is iodine-rich seaweed. In Switzerland, there is a high incidence of goiter, stemming from a lack of iodine. But in Japan there is hardly any incidence of this disease because of the high intake of fish, seaweed, and other seafood that is a part of the Japanese diet. The Japanese use more than five hundred different varieties of seaweed.

Iodine is water-soluble, and is found only in foods that grow within eighty miles of the ocean. Egg yolk contains a small amount of iodine, and onions, garlic, and leeks have it. Of course, all seafood contains some iodine. We have to be careful when cooking iodine-rich food in water, since it can be easily lost.

If you keep up your daily intake of iodine, you will be doing your body a great service. Iodine is necessary for controlling calcium in the body. For this reason alone you should make sure you get enough of it every day. Besides causing goiter, an iodine deficiency can lead to hypothyroidism, with many identifiable symptoms. You might also be interested in knowing that iodine-rich foods are great for your sex life!

Some delicatessens are beginning to stock different kinds of seaweed, such as dulse and nori. You can buy it in leaf form or cut up fine. It should be soaked ahead of time and put into the soup five minutes before it's done.

In addition to seaweed, I highly recommend putting parsley in soup. I don't add it until the soup is almost done, since parsley is good only when it is raw. It's very good for the kidneys, and we use it too much for decorative purposes and not enough as a food.

You can make a very healthy squash soup using banana squash, yellow crookneck squash, or hubbard squash. You can also make avocado soup if you like, but I would avoid this because avocado is better raw. Of course, you could put it into the soup after it is finished cooking.

You might try using green peppers in your soup. They are high in vitamin A. Or perhaps you can add apple peelings to your soup as a tonic for your kidneys.

The best root vegetable I know of is the beet—the greatest liver and gallbladder cleanser known to man. The Russian people of the Ukraine use beets a great deal, and they have the least amount of bowel trouble and bile disturbances. Studies in Switzerland have also shown that the nutritional value of the beet is very high. It is a great detoxifier of the liver and is slightly laxative.

If you want to shed some pounds, you can easily reduce the starch content of your soup. For example, you might eliminate the potatoes from your soup but keep the carrots, which are only 12 percent carbohydrate. You could also use rutabagas or turnips, since they are also 12 to 14 percent carbohydrate.

You should avoid putting Swiss chard or spinach into soups. I don't recommend using these because they contain large amounts of oxalic acid, which reduces the assimilation of calcium. A high intake of oxalic acid has a detrimental effect on the joints of the body.

Instead of taking nutritional supplements individually in pill form, try adding them directly to the soup just before it is served. They will be digested and assimilated much better that way. A green concentrate of chlorophyll is one such supplement that might be used, taking a teaspoon of this chlorophyll and adding it to the soup. And it is always beneficial to add chopped greens to your soup.

SOUP PREPARATION

When preparing your soup, it is a good idea to group together those ingredients that require the same cooking time. For example, you might cut up potatoes, carrots, and parsnips—all root vegetables. These can be cooked together with peas and celery, since they all take about the same amount of time to cook. This soup needs only to be simmered. There is nothing in it that requires heavy boiling. It is best not to make these vegetables too soft. Dentists are getting a lot of business these days from people who eat too many soft foods. It's better to leave soup ingredients a little chewy. Chewing is important, after all, since digestion starts in the mouth. I believe that stomach trouble, digestive disturbances, and gas are the result of not chewing properly.

Some of the soup ingredients may have to be timed, and different ones introduced at different times so that they will all be cooked properly. For example, potatoes should be added toward the end of the soup-making process so that they are not too soft, and peas take a bit longer to cook than tomatoes. On the other hand, overcooking vegetables will destroy their nutrients. Proper cooking is part of the art of soup-making and can be mastered with practice.

One way to handle vegetables that require a long cooking time is to run them through either a coarse or fine grater. This shortens the cooking time. Babies and some young children need their food grated fine. But you will find that you only have to cook vegetables for half the time when they are run through a grater first. This is especially true with beets. Beets take quite a while when steamed full size, but you can grate them and cut the cooking time down to a few minutes. Cabbage can also be made this way.

I don't suggest using aluminum cookware to prepare your soup. I prefer stainless steel because it is more resistant to acid and alkaline chemical reactions. We don't need to have aluminum dissolved from the cooking utensils in our foods.

There are three nutrient robbers in the kitchen: high heat, cooking in water, and exposure to air. Try to use cookware with tight-fitting lids, so that when you simmer soup you don't lose a lot of the steam.

Also keep in mind that it is very difficult to simmer on most electric ranges. Usually, a gas range is better.

Raw Liquefied Soups

Soup doesn't always have to be cooked. It you like, you can make delicious raw soups in your blender. I think one of the best soups you can have is raw asparagus soup. The asparagus can be run through the liquefier, added to a milk base or soy milk base, and then put into a pan for cooking. It can be flavored any way you like—using your vegetable broth powder, adding a little bit of cream at the table, or even adding a dash of butter.

You can make corn soup the same way—a raw corn soup so delicious that you have never really tasted corn until you have tasted it in this soup. After you have taken the corn off the cob, you may put it into a blender (if you wish to break it down a little bit more). Or you can leave it in whole kernels so it's nice and chewy. When you break the kernels off the corn cob, you will find that raw corn is very alkaline-forming. Once corn has been frozen or kept away from the cob for any length of time, it becomes a starch—very acid-forming.

You may want to try liquefying grains *after* they have been cooked—you will find that they can be used very nicely by adding greens and other vegetables to the soup. There is still another way of using the blender—that is to liquefy carrots and celery *before* cooking them. Then you won't have to cook the soup as long. With a little inventiveness, you will find many more raw soups that can be made quickly and easily in your blender.

Consistency

In your cooking program you should use as little water as possible. When the soup is cooked it shouldn't be runny, especially if it is intended as a meal in itself. Yet there is such a thing as making it *too* thick (like a goulash).

If you want to thin a soup, try adding a little stock, broth, or water. Or you might add almond or coconut milk instead. These have a thicker consistency than water, and also increase the soup's nutritional value. Or how about using raw vegetable juices? I wouldn't add these juices until *after* the soup has been cooked. I would add them at the table and use them as flavorings. Carrot juice can always be used very nicely in soup in place of carrots. There are many kinds of raw vegetable juices that you can use, ranging from cabbage juice to celery juice. If fresh vegetable juices are not available, you can try V-8, a canned vegetable juice, in your soup. It is a very good substitute for fresh juices.

When we steam spinach or string beans or squash, we often throw away the cooking water. But this cooking water contains all of the soluble salts we need. So it's a good idea to make your soup from this vegetable stock. Or you can use leftover cooked vegetables in broth to save some time. I highly recommend green kale with cooked barley, which can also be made raw. This is a high-calcium broth that is especially good for growing children.

You can use any kind of bran to thicken and add fiber to your soup. A good choice is oat bran, which is free of the gluten that is found in wheat, and is also high in fiber. Oat bran is a silicon food. Silicon keeps vitamin B in the body, and is good for the skin, hair, nails, and nervous system. If it were really cold outside and you wanted to derive a lot of calcium from your soup, you could add barley that has been cooked ahead of time instead of oat bran. Never add cereal grain last. In fact, you should cook it before you have cooked the vegetables.

If you want to thicken a soup at any time, add agar-agar, which can be purchased at a health food store.

Flavor

In addition to the vegetables themselves, herbal seasonings such as anise, thyme, and basil can be used to enhance a soup's flavor. Lots of people flavor their soups with herbs.

Another way of flavoring your soup is by using cayenne powder. I enjoy the flavor of Chinese parsley in many of my soups as well. It has a very strong taste, though, so use it sparingly.

Paprika and other spices are popular choices for enhancing flavor. If you prefer spices to herbs, try to select those that you know are not irritating to the digestive system.

In the final preparation of your soup, you may want to add a little soy sauce for flavoring. I never flavor with regular salt, nor do I add monosodium glutamate or other chemical flavorings. You can put in a little vegetable broth powder—a broth seasoning that you can find in a health food store.

Other alternatives for enriching your soup's flavor include almond butter and sesame seed butter. They can be mixed into soups or used on top. You don't even have to cook them. If you want to add a little butter to your soup, wait until after you sit down at the table.

SERVING SUGGESTIONS

As long as you are spending close to an hour preparing and cooking your soup, you might as well make enough for tomorrow or for another day. Soup keeps well for a day or two if refrigerated, and even longer if frozen. But if it is left to stand in a warm room, bacteria will begin to develop.

Soup may be served with other foods or it can be a whole meal itself. During its preparation, try to think of foods that will best complement your soup. You can prepare these dishes to accompany your soup at lunch or dinner meals.

If the soup is to accompany a protein meal, this main entrée should consist of meat, fish, cheese, or tofu. Always think about what you're putting into the soup. Make sure that it has enough calcium, iron, and—above all—greens. Soup greens are something that I feel has helped many of my patients.

If you want to make your soup a "whole" meal, you should keep in mind the following suggestions. Make sure that you have sufficient protein and carbohydrates to comply with your nutritional and caloric needs (400 to 600 calories) for a meal. If the soup is entirely vegetable, for example, it could be served with cheddar cheese sticks, cottage cheese, two slices of cold turkey, or some other protein that harmonizes well with the soup. A small, mixed green salad will provide the fresh, raw vegetables that you need (complex carbohydrates), and will serve as a wonderful complement to the soup, supplying the live enzymes, minerals, vitamins, and fiber that are so important. You may want to have a plate of fresh fruit instead of the tossed green salad, and a serving of cornbread or an oat bran muffin may make a nice complement to both soup and salad. Those who are more calorie-conscious may prefer to have Ry-Krisp, rice crackers, sesame crackers, or a thin slice of rye bread. I do not recommend wheat crackers or wheat bread, because the average American has far too much wheat in his diet.

Of course, the soup alone may contain an adequate amount of protein and complex carbohydrates to make it a "whole" meal—nutritionally balanced and sufficiently satisfying to require no additional foods.

SOME FINAL SUGGESTIONS

Your options for soup-making are limitless. In Denmark, fruit soups are popular. Fruit soups can be made from a prune base, for example, or from huckleberries. My mother used tapioca in her soup. Or you could use gelatin.

Another nice ingredient to use in soups is the mushroom. The Japanese have what they call a forest mushroom. It is a kind of flattened mushroom that measures two to three inches across the top. The directions given say you should soak it for twenty minutes and discard the stem. You may then slice it or cut it up any way you wish. You don't have to soak it if you don't want to; instead, you can add it to the soup when you first bring it to a simmer. By the time the soup is done, the mushrooms will be tender enough to eat.

Remember to use your imagination, and to love what you are doing, because the best ingredient in any prepared dish is always the love that goes into the making of it. Some of the soup recipes that I have collected are in the next chapter. They are a healthy addition to any meal, and some may be served alone. Enjoy!

5. MY FAVORITE SOUPS:
Savory Soups That Satisfy

Although soup has been around for centuries, its popularity has never really diminished. Delicious and satisfying, soup also promotes good health and harmony with nature. My travels have taken me all over the world, and everyone seems to be in agreement on this point.

I know you're going to love the recipes I've included here. I wouldn't be surprised if you decided to have soup for dinner this very night!

BARLEY SOUP

SERVES 2-3

2 cups unpearled barley
1 onion, chopped fine
1 cup celery, chopped fine
½ cup green pepper, chopped fine
2 carrots, diced
Vegetable seasoning (to taste)
1 Tbs. butter
1 Tbs. fresh cream

Soup may be blended and strained for a cream soup, if desired.

1. Soak barley overnight; cook until almost tender.
2. Add onion, celery, pepper, and carrots, along with more water (if necessary). Cook until tender.
3. Add vegetable seasoning.
4. Just prior to serving, add butter and cream.

MUSHROOM-BARLEY SOUP

SERVES 2

1 cup unpearled barley
3 cups vegetable broth
1 onion, sliced
1 turnip, chopped
1 cup tender young mushrooms, sliced
Vegetable seasoning (to taste)
Chopped parsley (as garnish)

Other vegetables used may include string beans, green soybeans, garbanzos, and green peas.

1. Soak barley overnight; cook until almost tender.
2. Drain off water. Add vegetable broth.
3. Add onion, carrot, and turnip. Cook until tender.
4. Drop in sliced mushrooms, and finish cooking.
5. As a final touch, add vegetable seasoning and sprinkle with parsley.

SERVES 4

CARROT AND GREEN BEAN SOUP

2 cups grated carrots
2 cups sliced green beans
4 cups vegetable broth
Vegetable seasoning (to taste)

1. Add carrots and green beans to vegetable broth.
2. Simmer until tender.
3. Season with vegetable seasoning.
4. Serve hot.

SERVES 6

BORSCH

4 cups shredded raw beets
3 cups shredded cabbage
½ cup sliced onion
1 cup sliced celery tops
1 bay leaf
6 cups vegetable broth or water
2 tsp. vegetable seasoning
2 Tbs. lemon juice
1 cup sour cream or plain yogurt

For taste variations, you may leave out the shredded cabbage or add 1 tablespoon of old-fashioned brown sugar, if desired.

1. Place first seven ingredients in a pot. Bring to a boil, then simmer for half an hour.
2. Strain. Discard vegetables.
3. Add lemon juice to liquid.
4. Heat to serving temperature only. Or, chill and serve cold.
5. Garnish each dish with a spoonful of sour cream or yogurt.

HAWAIIAN POTAGE   SERVES 4

1 potato, unpeeled and diced
¼ cup sliced mushrooms
1¼ cup sliced asparagus
Water (enough to cover vegetables)
1½ cups coconut milk
2 cups milk
Vegetable seasoning (to taste)

1. Place first four ingredients in a pot. Cook just until tender.
2. Pass through a coarse sieve.
3. Heat coconut milk and milk for about ten minutes, in a separate pot.
4. Combine mixtures, adding vegetable seasoning, and heat to serving temperature.

MINESTRONE   SERVES 4

½ cup bran water
1½ cups vegetable broth
1 clove garlic, crushed
1 medium-sized onion, chopped
1 cup celery, cut up
¼ cup parsley, chopped
¼ tsp. oregano
⅛ tsp. red pepper
2 medium-sized tomatoes, sliced
1½ cups finely-shredded cabbage
1 cup chick peas, cooked and drained
1 cup cooked, whole wheat macaroni
Grated Parmesan cheese

1. Place first eight ingredients in a covered saucepan. Bring to a boil and simmer for fifteen minutes.
2. Add next four ingredients. Simmer all ingredients in saucepan for another ten minutes.
3. Serve with grated Parmesan cheese.

SERVES 4

ITALIAN PARMESAN SOUP

1 qt. vegetable consommé
4 Tbs. grated Parmesan cheese
1 cup whole grain bread crumbs
2 eggs, slightly beaten
Vegetable seasoning (to taste)

Vegetable consommé is the broth obtained by straining the liquid from fresh vegetables that were brought to a boil in water, and then simmered for approximately twenty minutes. Any combination of vegetables may be used. (Onions are often included for flavor.) Consommé is rich in vitamins and minerals.

1. Heat vegetable consommé.
2. Stir cheese, bread crumbs, and eggs into boiling consommé.
3. Season with vegetable seasoning and serve immediately.

SERVES 2

MUSHROOM SOUP

½ lb. chopped mushrooms
4 Tbs. butter
½ cup chopped celery
¼ cup chopped onion
⅛ cup chopped parsley
⅛ cup finely-sliced carrots
2 cups stock or water
2 tsp. vegetable seasoning

1. Sauté mushrooms in butter.
2. Add next five ingredients and simmer for twenty minutes. Purée through sieve.
3. Add vegetable seasoning and serve.

Super Soups

I like to use some special natural ingredients in my soups to increase their nutritional value, to thicken, or to enhance flavor. The following, available in most natural food stores, are a few of my favorites.

- *Apple concentrate:* A preparation of whole fruit by low heat; rich in minerals and natural sugars.
- *Arrowroot powder:* An alkaline flour high in calcium, better than wheat and corn flours as a thickening agent.
- *Bran water:* A high mineral solution made by simmering wheat bran in water to extract water-soluble nutrients.
- *Coconut milk:* A highly nutritious "milk" made by steeping or liquefying fresh, shredded coconut in warm water and squeezing through muslin. Also obtainable in powder form.
- *Dulse:* A powdered Nova Scotia seaweed high in iodine and manganese.
- *Gelatin:* A good source of protein and joint-nourishing nutrients.
- *Herbs:* Concentrated "original" plants of high nutritive value and useful as flavorings and seasonings.
- *Herb teas:* Extracts of different herbs obtained by steeping pieces of the plant (usually dried, crumbled) in boiling water.

- *Oat straw tea:* A high silicon tea made from oat straw. It should be boiled for twenty minutes to extract the silicon.
- *Paprika:* A powder made by grinding the dried ripe fruit of a variety of capsicum. A tasty seasoning, high in vitamins A and C.
- *Vegetable bouillon cubes:* Flavorful cubes made from vegetable extracts, useful in stock and soup-making. Some are imitation meat-flavored.
- *Vegetable broth or stock:* Juices obtained or left over after cooking vegetables (free from meat juices). For a more flavorful stock, try adding fresh or dried herbs, or onion, garlic, or leeks. If the stock won't be used immediately, bring it to a boil, cool, and refrigerate. It will keep for three to four days.
- *Vegetable powders:* Various vegetables, such as celery, onion, and okra, that are dehydrated by careful methods to obtain nutritious powdered vegetables.
- *Vegetable seasoning:* A concentrate of tasty dry-powdered or flaked raw vegetables, high in minerals and amino acids. A delicious "salty" seasoning.
- *Whey powder:* A handy form of whey made from the liquid left over from cheese-making. High in sodium.

ONION CONSOMME　SERVES 4

6 large, sliced onions
4 cups oat straw tea or water
¼ cup vegetable seasoning
Butter (to taste)
Parsley (as garnish)

1. Simmer onions and tea (or water) until onions are tender. Strain.
2. Add vegetable seasoning and butter to liquid.
3. Garnish with parsley and serve.

SERVES 3-4   # SPINACH-MUSHROOM SOUP

2 cups fresh spinach
1 cup sliced mushrooms
1 small onion, cut up
1/2 tsp. vegetable seasoning
1/2 cup vegetable broth or herb tea
1/4 tsp. nutmeg
Shake of paprika
2 cups milk
1 Tbs. butter

1. Cook first seven ingredients very gently for five minutes. Purée.
2. Add milk.
3. Serve either hot or cold, stirring in butter just before removing from saucepan.

SERVES 4   # COOL POTATO SOUP

4 sliced potatoes
1 large onion, sliced
2/3 cup potato water
2 Tbs. butter
Milk (enough to adjust consistency)
2 tsp. vegetable seasoning
1 tsp. turmeric
1 large cucumber, coarsely shredded
Chopped chives (as garnish)

1. Cook potatoes and onion in very little water.
2. Rub through sieve or blender to purée with potato water and butter.
3. Add milk to adjust consistency.
4. Add vegetable seasoning and turmeric, and chill.
5. Add shredded cucumber and garnish with chopped chives before serving.

SWEET POTATO SOUP

SERVES 2

2 cooked sweet potatoes, mashed
1 cup milk
Chopped chives (as garnish)

1. Blend potatoes and milk until smooth. Heat without boiling.
2. Garnish with chopped chives.

Thermos Soups

The wide-mouthed thermos flask is a great aid to soup-making. Cube your vegetables finely and simmer in stock for five minutes to heat them through. Preheat the thermos with a little boiling water, quickly pour in the boiling soup, and put the lid on tightly. If you do this in the morning, by evening you will have a delicious soup that's ready to serve—of the right temperature, cooked gently and healthfully, and at no risk of overcooking. Grated soup vegetables need to be brought to a boil only before being poured into your thermos to cook. Season with vegetable bouillon cubes, vegetable powders, herbs, onion, and garlic. Add a little butter or cream just before serving, if so desired.

Legume soups, which boil over so easily, are made without fuss in the thermos. Prepare the ingredients as usual, soak the legumes overnight, and pre-cook all of the ingredients for about five minutes. Then pour the ingredients into your hot thermos, cork, and let stand for approximately eight hours to cook.

Soup can be thermos-cooked even more quickly if your soybeans or lentils are soaked overnight and then ground in a liquefier before cooking. Bring to a boil and seal in the thermos. Or dry-grind your legumes to a powder, place in hot thermos with minced onion, celery, and seasoning, pour in your boiling stock, and give a gentle stir to mix before closing. In three or four hours, your soup will be cooked.

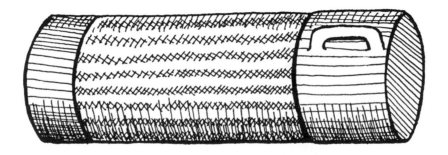

SERVES 2

SOPA DE QUESO

½ ripe tomato
½ sliced onion
½ bay leaf
¼ tsp. paprika
¼ tsp. cinnamon
3 cups seasoned vegetable stock or water
½ cup green spinach noodles
1 egg
1 Tbs. butter
1 Tbs. olive oil
½ cup finely-grated Edam cheese
Whole wheat noodles

1. Slice tomato and stew in small amount of water over very gentle heat.
2. Add onion and bay leaf and cook slowly for a few minutes, covered.
3. Add paprika, cinnamon, and vegetable stock (or water) and cook for fifteen minutes.
4. Carefully pour off two cups of the broth into another saucepan. Add green spinach noodles to broth and cook until tender.
5. In bowl, beat egg, butter, and olive oil with an egg beater.
6. Add thick soup (remove bay leaf) and beat until smooth.
7. Stir in Edam cheese.
8. Pour onto hot noodles and serve immediately.

SPANISH SUMMER SOUP

SERVES 2

1¹/₂ cups tomatoes, chopped
¹/₄ cup celery, chopped
¹/₄ cup cucumbers, chopped
2 Tbs. onion, chopped
¹/₂ green pepper, chopped
¹/₄ cup cooked beets, chopped
1 clove garlic, crushed
¹/₃ cup whole wheat bread crumbs
1 tsp. paprika
¹/₂ tsp. basil
¹/₄ tsp. cloves, ground
2 tsp. vegetable seasoning
¹/₄ cup lemon juice
³/₄ cup vegetable broth
2 Tbs. safflower oil

1. Combine first six ingredients.
2. Add garlic, bread crumbs, paprika, basil, cloves, and vegetable seasoning and mix well.
3. Add lemon juice, vegetable broth, and safflower oil, and stir thoroughly. Chill and serve as a cold soup.

Making Your Own Croutons

Croutons are great for adding variety, interest, and crunch to your soups and salads. You can buy whole grain croutons at your health food store, or—just as easily—you can make your own.

The best croutons—those with the crunchiest texture—are made from stale bread. If you don't have any stale bread on hand, though, use fresh bread, and leave the croutons in the oven a little longer. Any whole grain bread will do, whether rye, pumpernickel, whole wheat, or another bread of your choosing. For maximum nutrition and flavor, though, you'll want to avoid any breads made with bleached white flour.

If you are short on time, you can make croutons by popping a slice of bread in the toaster. (One slice of bread makes about ³/₄ cup.) When the toast is done, use a sharp knife to cut it quickly into cubes or squares, and use immediately.

If you have a little more time, make your croutons in the oven. Before baking, cut the bread in ¹/₂-inch cubes, or, for fun, use small cookie cutters to make stars or rounds. Spread the croutons on a shallow baking pan, and bake in a preheated 300°F oven for thirty minutes, or until the bread is dry and golden. Use the croutons immediately, or store for a few days in a moisture-proof container.

SERVES 4

TOMATO SOUP

1 cup water
½ cup onion, diced
¼ cup green pepper, diced
¼ cup celery, finely chopped
Vegetable seasoning (to taste)
3 cups fresh tomato juice
Arrowroot (as a thickening agent)
¼ cup lemon juice
Brown sugar (to taste)

1. Combine water, onion, pepper, celery, and vegetable seasoning. Cook until tender.
2. Add tomato juice and heat through.
3. Thicken with arrowroot. For variation, add some brown rice to the soup and cook, instead of adding arrowroot. Add lemon juice and brown sugar for flavoring.
4. For a garnish, add leftover green pepper, chopped finely.

SERVES 2

TOMATO-ASPARAGUS SOUP

1 cup water
½ bay leaf
2 cups solid-packed tomatoes
¾ cup asparagus
2 Tbs. finely-chopped onion
2 tsp. vegetable seasoning
Fresh cream (enough to adjust consistency)
Chopped parsley (as garnish)

1. Simmer first six ingredients together for thirty minutes; strain or blend until smooth.
2. Reheat in a double boiler. When hot enough to serve, add cream.
3. Serve immediately with a garnish of chopped parsley.

TOMATO OKRA SOUP

SERVES 4

1 cup sliced okra
1/2 cup water
3 cups tomato purée
2 cups thick Nut Milk or Sesame Seed Milk (below)
3 Tbs. vegetable seasoning
2 Tbs. butter

1. Cook okra in water until tender.
2. Add tomato purée, Nut Milk or Sesame Seed Milk, and vegetable seasoning.
3. Heat to serving temperature. Stir in butter and serve immediately.

NUT OR SESAME SEED MILK

MAKES 1 QUART

1/2 cup raw, hulled almonds or 1/3 cup raw, hulled sesame seeds
(other nuts or seeds may be used, if preferred)

1. Put almonds or sesame seeds in a one-quart container.
2. Add water.
3. Soak at least 8 hours.
4. Just before serving, liquefy and strain. Use only the liquid.

SERVES 4

VEGETABLE BROTH DELIGHT

1 cup okra, cut up
1 cup string beans, sliced
½ cup carrots, diced
2 turnips, diced
1 large onion, sliced
½ cup celery, cut up
½ cup peas
1 clove garlic, crushed
1 Tbs. vegetable seasoning
2 cups tomato juice
Fresh cream (if desired)

1. Steam all ingredients until tender.
2. A little cream may be added at the table, if desired.

SERVES 6-8

VEGETABLE SOUP— VARIATION I

3 cups chopped onion
3 cups chopped celery
3 large green peppers, chopped
½ head cabbage, chopped
1 Tbs. vegetable seasoning
Herbs (to taste)
2 cups stewed or canned tomatoes
2 cups tomato juice
1 cup chopped watercress or parsley

1. Cover first six ingredients with water or broth and cook over low heat until vegetables are tender.
2. Add tomatoes, tomato juice, and watercress (or parsley) and heat through. Serve.

VEGETABLE SOUP— VARIATION II

SERVES 2

½ cup diced celery
¼ cup diced celery root
¼ cup sliced onions
½ cup diced parsnips
Fresh dill
2½ cups water
Vegetable seasoning (to taste)
½ cup parsley
2 cloves garlic
Pat butter
Alfalfa sprouts (as garnish)

1. Bring first seven ingredients to a boil, then simmer until tender.
2. Remove a quarter of the vegetables and liquefy or sieve to act as a thickening agent.
3. Liquefy parsley and garlic in some of the broth.
4. Stir into soup well and add butter.
5. Garnish with alfalfa sprouts.

WHITE VEGETABLE SOUP

SERVES 3-4

2 potatoes, diced
1 parsnip, diced
1 turnip, diced
1 onion, coarsely sliced
1 leek (white part), sliced
1 bay leaf
Other herbs (as desired)
¾ tsp. sea salt
Water (enough to cover)
Chopped parsley (as garnish)

1. Bring first nine ingredients to a boil and simmer until tender.
2. Garnish with chopped parsley.

SERVES 4

THICK VEGETABLE SOUP

1 cup corn (off cob)
½ cup chopped onion
½ cup diced eggplant
1 stalk celery, diced
1 small green pepper, diced
2 cups diced potatoes
3 tsp. vegetable seasoning
Herb seasoning of your choice (to taste)
3½ cups vegetable broth
Vegetable bouillon cube (if desired)
Agar-agar (as a thickening agent)
2 Tbs. butter
Tomato juice (to adjust consistency)

1. Bring first nine ingredients to a boil, then simmer gently until tender.
2. Add a vegetable bouillon cube for flavoring, if desired.
3. Thicken with a little agar–agar at end of cooking time.
4. Stir in butter.
5. Use tomato juice to adjust consistency, if necessary.

SERVES 3-4

VICHYSSOISE

1 cup diced, raw potatoes (unpeeled)
¼ cup sliced green onions
1½ cups water
1½ tsp. vegetable seasoning
1 cup raw peas
½ cup diced celery
1 cup heavy cream
Chopped chives (as garnish)

1. Cook first six ingredients until tender. Cool.
2. Purée through a sieve.
3. Blend in heavy cream.
4. Serve chilled with chopped chives as garnish.

CREAM SOUPS

CREAM OF CARROT SOUP   SERVES 4

1 medium-sized onion, sliced
2 cups carrots, diced
2 tsp. vegetable seasoning
2 cups vegetable stock
1 cup thick Sesame Seed Milk (page 103)
2 Tbs. butter
Alfalfa sprouts (as garnish)

1. Cook first four ingredients gently until tender; pass through strainer.
2. Add Sesame Seed Milk and butter.
3. Heat to serving temperature only.
4. Serve with a garnish of alfalfa sprouts.

CARROT-CHEESE CREAM SOUP   SERVES 3-4

2 cups milk
1 slice onion, chopped
4 medium-sized carrots, cut up
1½ tsp. vegetable seasoning
¼ tsp. red pepper
3 Tbs. butter
1 cup grated, hard cheddar cheese
Parsley (as garnish)

1. Place first five ingredients in a saucepan. Bring to a boil and simmer until tender. Purée.
2. Stir in butter and cheese.
3. Add a little more milk if thinning is necessary.
4. Garnish with parsley.

SERVES 4

CREAM OF CORN CHOWDER

1 cup corn (off cob)
1½ cups diced, unpeeled potatoes
¼ cup chopped onion
2 tsp. vegetable seasoning
1½ cups mint tea or water
1 cup stewed tomatoes
1 cup milk
1 cup fresh cream

1. Cook first five ingredients until tender.
2. Add tomatoes, and heat to serving temperature.
3. Heat milk and cream and add upon serving.

SERVES 2

CREAM OF LIMA SOUP

1 pkg. frozen baby limas (green)
⅓ cup green onions or scallions, chopped
½ tsp. marjoram, fresh or dried
4 sprigs of parsley
Shake of red pepper
1 tsp. vegetable seasoning
1½ cups vegetable water or broth
½ cup milk or fresh cream
Chopped parsley or chives (as garnish)

1. Cook first seven ingredients gently until tender. Purée.
2. Gradually blend in milk or cream.
3. Serve either hot or cold, garnishing with chopped parsley or chives.

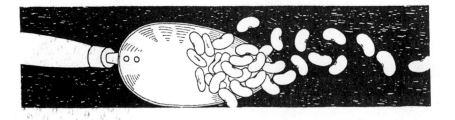

CREAM OF MUSHROOM SOUP SERVES 4

½ lb. fresh, chopped mushrooms
2 cups vegetable stock
3 beaten egg yolks
1 cup fresh cream

1. Simmer mushrooms and vegetable stock until tender.
2. Place mixture in double boiler, and stir in egg yolks.
3. Cook very gently, stirring until thickened.
4. Add cream, and serve.

CREAM OF OKRA SOUP SERVES 2

1 cup sliced tomatoes
1 cup sliced okra
1 slice onion
2 tsp. vegetable seasoning
½ cup broth or water
2 tsp. arrowroot
1 tsp. raw sugar
1 Tbs. water
1 cup fresh cream

1. Cook first five ingredients gently until tender. Purée through a sieve or in a blender.
2. Mix arrowroot, sugar, and water to a cream. Stir into soup over heat to thicken.
3. Add fresh cream, and serve.

SERVES 4

CREAM OF PARSNIP SOUP

2 cups parsnips, diced
1 medium-sized onion, sliced
2 cups vegetable stock
1 tsp. vegetable seasoning
1 Tbs. raw sugar
½ cup fine, whole grain bread crumbs
1 cup milk
4 Tbs. fresh cream
Chopped chives (as garnish)

1. Cook first five ingredients until tender. Pass through a strainer.
2. Add bread crumbs and milk and heat gently until serving temperature is reached.
3. Stir in cream, garnish with chopped chives, and serve.

SERVES 4

CREAM OF VEGETABLE SOUP

3 Tbs. butter
2 Tbs. arrowroot
3 cups milk
2 Tbs. vegetable seasoning
1 tsp. onion juice
2 cups mixed vegetables, puréed
Chopped chives and paprika (as garnish)

1. Melt butter over low heat.
2. Add arrowroot, and continue cooking over low heat for three to five minutes, stirring constantly.
3. Stir milk in slowly to complete white sauce. Then add vegetable seasoning, onion juice, and puréed vegetables. Heat mixture through.
4. Serve with a garnish of chopped chives and paprika.

CREAM OF ONION SOUP

SERVES 3-4

2½ cups sliced onion
2 potatoes, cubed
2 cups vegetable broth
3 tsp. vegetable seasoning
2 Tbs. butter
1 Tbs. chopped parsley
Milk or fresh cream (as a thickening agent)

1. Simmer first four ingredients until tender. Rub through a sieve. Re-heat.
2. Stir in butter and parsley.
3. Use milk or cream to thicken, and serve.

LEGUME SOUPS

The legume family includes lentils, peas, and beans. These are high in B-complex vitamins and carbohydrates, with a modest amount of high-quality protein. Legumes are "energy foods" for people who are physically active, who work hard, and who enjoy life!

BASIC LEGUME SOUP

SERVES 2

½ cup beans (or other legumes)
2 cups vegetable broth or herb tea
2 sprigs mint or another suitable herb
Vegetable seasoning (to taste)
½ tsp. dulse powder
½ onion, sliced
2 Tbs. butter or fresh cream
Chopped parsley or chives (as garnish)

1. Simmer first six ingredients gently until tender. Purée. Heat to serving temperature.
2. Stir in butter or cream.
3. Garnish with chopped parsley or chives, and serve.

SERVES 4

BEAN-CELERY SOUP

1 cup beans, soaked overnight
3 cups vegetable broth
½ cup chopped celery
¼ cup sliced onion
Choice of herb (as seasoning)
2 Tbs. butter
3 tsp. vegetable seasoning
Finely-chopped green pepper (as garnish)

1. Cook first five ingredients until tender.
2. Add butter and vegetable seasoning.
3. Rub through a strainer or blend until smooth in a pre-heated liquefier. Avoid re-heating, if possible.
4. Serve in warmed soup dishes and garnish with green pepper.

SERVES 4

BEAN-TOMATO SOUP

1 cup kidney beans
3 cups water
1 cup chopped onion
¼ cup chopped green pepper
1 small bay leaf
2 cups chopped tomatoes
1 Tbs. soy sauce
2 tsp. vegetable seasoning

1. Cook first five ingredients until almost tender.
2. Add tomatoes, soy sauce, and vegetable seasoning, and simmer until tender.

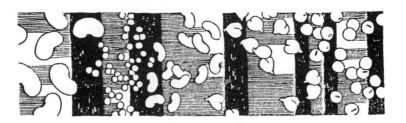

SOYBEAN SOUP   SERVES 3

1 cup soybeans
6 small, whole onions
Vegetable seasoning (to taste)

1. Soak beans overnight in water.
2. Combine with onions, adding more water if necessary.
3. Cook until beans are soft. Remove onions.
4. Grind beans, using the bean liquid, until a good soup consistency is obtained.
2. Season with vegetable seasoning and serve hot.

SOY TOMATO SOUP   SERVES 2

2 cups cooked soybeans
1 cup cooked onions, carrots, and celery
Tomato juice (to correct consistency)
1 Tbs. butter
Vegetable seasoning (to taste)
Dash of paprika

1. Put soybeans, onions, carrots, and celery through a sieve, using tomato juice to correct consistency.
2. Add butter, vegetable seasoning, and paprika, and heat to serving temperature.

SERVES 6

KIDNEY BEAN SOUP

2 cups cooked and puréed kidney beans
6 vegetable bouillon cubes
1 onion, finely minced
2 cups celery juice or broth
4 cups bean liquid
2 Tbs. butter
Vegetable seasoning (to taste)
Onion rings (as garnish)

1. Heat first seven ingredients in a double boiler until serving temperature is reached.
2. Garnish with onion rings, and serve.

SERVES 3

LIMA BEAN SOUP

3 cups anise tea (or another of your choice)
1 cup baby limas
1 tsp. paprika
3 cloves garlic, crushed
½ cup chopped parsley
Vegetable seasoning (to taste)

1. Cook first five ingredients until tender.
2. Blend in liquefier (or purée through a sieve) one-third of the mixture. Use as a thickening agent for the soup.
3. Season with vegetable seasoning and garnish with leftover chopped parsley. Serve.

THICK, BLACK-EYED PEA SOUP

SERVES 4

1 cup black-eyed peas
4 sliced tomatoes
1 sliced onion
1 clove garlic, chopped fine
1 Tbs. sesame oil
2 tsp. vegetable seasoning
Milk or Sesame Seed Milk (to correct consistency; page 103)

1. Soak peas overnight.
2. Add tomatoes, onion, and garlic, and simmer all together until tender.
3. Purée mixture.
4. Bring to a boil. Remove from stove.
5. Add sesame oil and vegetable seasoning.
6. Add milk or Sesame Seed Milk. Serve immediately in hot dishes.

SPLIT PEA SOUP

SERVES 2

½ cup split green peas
1½ cups oat straw tea or water
1-2 bay leaves
½ tsp. dulse
2 tsp. vegetable seasoning
1 small onion, chopped
2 sprigs mint
2 cloves garlic, crushed
1 lettuce leaf
Butter or fresh cream (to taste)

1. Cook first three ingredients until almost tender.
2. Add next six ingredients and cook until very soft.
3. Purée through a strainer or in a blender, adding a little butter or cream just before serving.

SERVES 6-8

CREAMED SPLIT PEA SOUP

1 lb. split peas
2 quarts water
1 bay leaf
2 cloves garlic
½ cup chopped onions
1 cup chopped celery with leaves
1 cup chopped carrots
¼ tsp. thyme
3 Tbs. vegetable seasoning
1 cup heavy cream

1. Soak split peas in water overnight.
2. Add bay leaf and garlic and simmer for one hour. Skim water while cooking. Remove bay leaf.
3. Add onions, celery, carrots, thyme, and vegetable seasoning. Cook for another half hour.
4. Purée mixture.
5. Add heavy cream and serve immediately.

SERVES 4

GREEN PEA SOUP

1 cup dry, split green peas
½ head cabbage
3 onions
2 Tbs. raisins
Vegetable seasoning (to taste)
Butter (to taste)

1. Soak peas overnight.
2. Chop up cabbage and onions fine. Keep raisins whole.
3. Simmer peas, cabbage, onions, raisins, and water to cover until vegetables are tender. Pass through a strainer or liquefier.
4. Season with vegetable seasoning and serve with a dot of butter in each bowl.

DUTCH PEA SOUP

SERVES 6–8

2 lbs. fresh veal joints
3 quarts water
1 Tbs. vegetable seasoning
1/2 tsp. red pepper
1/4 tsp. ground allspice
1/4 tsp. marjoram
1 vegetable bouillon cube
1 lb. split green peas
2 medium-sized leeks
1 large onion
1 cup celery, diced
Whole wheat bread croutons (page 101)

1. Simmer veal joints in water for one hour.
2. Add next six ingredients and simmer for an hour more.
3. Wash and slice leeks, and add to soup.
4. Peel and cut onion into rings. Add.
5. Add diced celery.
6. Simmer for another half hour, remove veal joints, and skim off fat. Serve with croutons.

LENTIL SOUP

SERVES 6

1/2 cup lentils
1/2 cup chopped onions
6 cups vegetable broth
1 bay leaf
3/4 cup soy noodles
1/4 cup sour cream
2 Tbs. vegetable oil
Vegetable seasoning (to taste)
Chopped parsley (as garnish)

1. Cook first four ingredients gently, stirring occasionally until vegetables are tender.
2. Add noodles, and simmer until done.
3. Add sour cream and vegetable oil just before removing from heat.
4. Season with vegetable seasoning and garnish with chopped parsley.

SERVES 3-4

LENTIL AND TOMATO SOUP

2 cups cooked lentils
2 cups stewed tomatoes
1 cup steamed millet
1 cup fresh cream
½ tsp. onion juice
2 tsp. vegetable seasoning
Onion rings (as garnish)

1. Purée lentils and tomatoes through a sieve.
2. Add millet, cream, onion juice, and vegetable seasoning. If necessary, add water to correct consistency.
3. Heat to serving temperature and garnish with onion rings.

SERVES 3-4

CREAM OF LENTIL SOUP

1 small onion, chopped fine
1 clove garlic, crushed
3 cups water or broth
1 cup yellow or green lentils
Milk or fresh cream (to thin)
Vegetable seasoning (to taste)
Butter (as garnish)
Parsley (as garnish)

1. Put onion, garlic, water (or broth), and lentils in a saucepan. Cook until soft.
2. Add milk or cream to thin.
3. Season with vegetable seasoning.
4. Heat without boiling.
5. Garnish each serving with a pat of butter and parsley just prior to serving.

NUT SOUPS

ASPARAGUS-NUT SOUP

SERVES 2

1 cup minced asparagus
2 cups mint tea or water
2 Tbs. nut butter
2 Tbs. warm milk

1. Combine asparagus (using lower part of spears, if desired) and mint tea (or water). Simmer gently for twenty minutes.
2. Rub through a sieve or blend. Re-heat.
3. Stir in nut butter and milk. Serve immediately.

CHESTNUT SOUP

SERVES 4

1 qt. oat straw tea or water
1 tsp. vegetable seasoning
1 small clove garlic
1 bay leaf
Pinch thyme
1 clove
1/2 stalk celery, diced
1/2 chili pepper, sliced
1 vegetable bouillon cube
1/4 cup potato flour
1/2 cup water
2 cups boiled chestnuts, peeled and chopped
1/2 cup fresh cream
1 egg

1. Simmer first eight ingredients for one hour.
2. Add and dissolve bouillon cube.
3. In separate bowl, mix potato flour and water until smooth. Add to soup to thicken stock. Strain.
4. Add chestnuts.
5. In a bowl, beat together egg and cream.
6. Bring soup almost to a boil. Remove from heat.
7. Whisk in egg and cream. Serve immediately.

SERVES 4

PEANUT BUTTER SOUP

3 Tbs. raw peanut butter
Juice of one lemon
4 cups milk
1 apple, finely grated
Pinch of cinnamon, nutmeg, or ginger for flavor

1. Soften peanut butter by adding lemon to it. Set aside.
2. Heat milk without boiling.
3. Stir in peanut butter mixture and heat gently for fifteen minutes.
4. Beat in apple and cinnamon, nutmeg, or ginger.
5. Serve hot in heated bowls.

SERVES 4

PEANUT SOUP

1/2 cup peanuts, ground to a meal
1 slice of onion, minced
3 Tbs. butter or olive oil
2 1/2 Tbs. arrowroot
Vegetable seasoning (to taste)
3 cups vegetable stock
1 cup heavy cream
1 egg yolk
1/3 cup peanuts, chopped (as garnish)

1. Combine first five ingredients in double boiler.
2. Gradually stir in vegetable stock.
3. Cook, stirring until thick. Remove from heat.
4. Mix cream and egg yolk together and stir into soup.
5. Garnish with chopped peanuts, and serve.

NUT BUTTER SOUP

SERVES **4**

2 cups hot milk
4 Tbs. nut butter or tahini
1/2 cup apple juice
Lemon rind
Pinch of cinnamon or nutmeg
Vegetable seasoning (to taste)
Dash of lemon juice

1. Beat all ingredients together with an egg beater.
2. Serve immediately in hot soup dishes.

SESAME PEANUT SOUP

SERVES **2**

2 cups Sesame Seed Milk (page 103)
2 Tbs. peanut butter
1/2 apple, grated very finely
1 Tbs. lemon juice
Grated lemon rind
Pinch of cinnamon and nutmeg
Grated peanut (as garnish)

1. Heat Sesame Seed Milk. Do not allow to boil.
2. Place next five ingredients in a hot mixing bowl. Pour in hot milk, whisking well.
3. Serve immediately in hot soup dishes, garnishing with a shake of grated peanut.

SERVES 3-4

NUT TOMATO SOUP

⅓ cup raw peanut butter
1 Tbs. minced green onion
1 Tbs. minced green pepper
1 Tbs. minced parsley
1-2 tsp. vegetable seasoning
4 cups tomato purée

1. Combine first five ingredients.
2. Add tomato purée gradually to other ingredients, stirring until smooth. Serve hot or cold.

SERVES 4-6

CREAM OF NUT SOUP

2 cups almonds, blanched if desired
3½ cups rich vegetable stock
Vegetable seasoning (to taste)
½ small onion, chopped
4 egg yolks
½ tsp. ground coriander
1 cup heavy cream, warmed
Minced chives (as garnish)
Finely-grated orange (as garnish)
Dash of soy sauce

If desired, cashews or pecans may be substituted for almonds.

1. Grind almonds into a meal. Set aside.
2. In a double boiler, bring vegetable stock, vegetable seasoning, and onion to a boil. Stir until smooth. Continue to cook gently, stirring until thick. Remove from heat.
3. Beat together egg yolks, coriander, and heavy cream.
4. Stir heavy cream mixture into soup, add almond meal, and serve in hot soup bowls garnished with minced chives and finely-grated orange for zest. A dash of soy sauce makes a nice finishing touch.

CHEESE SOUPS

Cheddar, Swiss, Gruyère, Roquefort, Parmesan, and Romano are just a few of the cheeses that can be used to add flavor and nutrients to your soups. Choose the one that you prefer, and adjust the seasoning to suit.

SIMPLE CHEESE SOUP

SERVES 3-4

2 cups vegetable broth, already boiled
1/2 onion, sliced
1/2 clove garlic, if desired
2 tsp. vegetable seasoning
Sprigs of parsley
1 1/2 cups grated cheese

1. Simmer first five ingredients until onion and garlic are tender.
2. Stir in grated cheese.
3. Pour into hot soup bowls, and serve.

PEA-CHEESE SOUP

SERVES 2

1 cup water from peas
1 cup mint tea
4 Tbs. cooked peas
1/2 onion, grated
2 tsp. vegetable seasoning
1/2 tsp. dulse powder
1 cup grated cheese

1. Bring first six ingredients to a boil.
2. Stir in grated cheese, and serve.

SERVES 3-4

CHEESE MILK SOUP

1½ cups cubed cheddar
2 cups very hot milk
1 clove garlic, chopped
Dash of nutmeg
Dash of paprika
2 tsp. vegetable seasoning
1 vegetable bouillon cube
1 egg yolk
Sprinkle of wheat germ
Chopped parsley (as garnish)

1. Blend first eight ingredients together in a pre-heated blender until smooth and creamy.
2. Serve in hot soup bowls with wheat germ. Add chopped parsley for color.

SERVES 3-4

MIXED VEGETABLE CHEESE SOUP

2 cups herb tea
1 cup sliced vegetables (of your own choosing)
2 tsp. vegetable seasoning
½ tsp. dulse powder
1 cup grated cheese
¼ cup safflower oil

1. Bring first four ingredients to a boil and simmer until tender. (All vegetables can be used raw if blending in liquefier.)
2. Beat cheese and oil in thoroughly or blend in liquefier.
3. Pour into hot soup bowls and serve immediately.

ROQUEFORT CHEESE SOUP

SERVES 2

2 cups herb tea or vegetable broth
½ onion, sliced
4 Tbs. crumbled Roquefort
4 Tbs. fresh cream
Dash of paprika (as garnish)

1. Bring herb tea or vegetable broth to a boil.
2. Combine with onion and Roquefort. Place in **pre-heated** blender, and blend until smooth.
3. Add cream, and blend briefly.
4. Serve in hot bowls with a dash of paprika **as garnish.**

BLENDED SOUPS

A blender—or liquefier, as it's sometimes called—will help you to make smooth, delicious, healthful soups in record time. Just follow a few simple rules (see page 126), and success will be yours!

A SIMPLE BORSCH

SERVES 1-2

½ small lemon, peeled and seeded
1 tsp. vegetable seasoning
1 cup diced, cooked beets
1 cup beet juice
½ cup sour cream
Sour cream (as garnish)

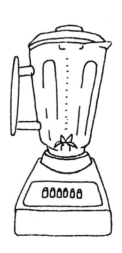

1. Blend first four ingredients until velvety smooth.
2. If soup is to be served cold, add half-cup of sour **cream to** mixture and blend until smooth.
3. If soup is to be served hot, remove mixture from blender and heat in saucepan until serving temperature is reached. Return heated mixture to blender, add half-cup sour cream, and blend until smooth.
4. Garnish with additional sour cream, and serve.

Blended Soups

A blender is practically a "must" for the health-conscious person these days and is a great timesaver as well. Novices should, however, observe a few helpful tips. Add solids first—always. Never fill the blender hopper more than half full. Make sure the cover is on before pressing the start button, and always begin at "low" or "slow" to avoid splattering. Once the ingredients are moving at low speed, you can remove the top and begin adding liquid ingredients—not too much at a time.

To test for appropriate taste and consistency, *turn off the blender first*, then insert spoon. *Never put a spoon into a running blender!* If you drop the spoon (and most people do, sooner or later), you'll ruin the blender.

To thicken the soup, add solids or a teaspoon of arrowroot powder. To thin the soup, add more liquid.

It is best not to pour boiling hot ingredients into a blender hopper (unless the manufacturer's instructions say you can).

The blender makes possible a new array of health soups—the raw soups. Just blend raw vegetables with a suitable liquid and seasoning, and serve either chilled or hot. The rawest of raw soups can be made very appetizing by using vegetable juices for the base, and vegetable seasoning, herbs, or various cheeses for flavor. Blend until smooth, chill, and serve garnished with parsley or mint leaves; celery juice with cheddar cheese and a little dill weed; tomato juice, cottage cheese, and basil, marjoram, or oregano. Or you can blend the ingredients and then warm the soup or cook it in a double boiler.

You can make tasty soups in your blender from odds and ends of leftover cooked vegetables and their juices. Add an onion and some vegetable seasoning for extra appeal. Do not recook; just heat it through.

With a blender, a cream soup can be created in a short time—smooth, delicious, healthful. It can be made as simply as possible by adding milk or cream to a plain vegetable soup and blending until smooth and creamy. Cooked vegetables can be liquefied with milk, cream, or an arrowroot white sauce, blended smooth, then heated to serving temperature (or chilled briefly for a cool soup). If using mostly milk, add a little butter to the hot soup for extra creaminess. Raw vegetables can be blended with milk or cream to make a nutritious, uncooked soup. Or try using nut milk for a change.

Blending before cooking greatly reduces the cooking time for legumes. Blended after cooking, a smooth, thick soup can be made very quickly and easily. Liquefying legumes aids in their digestion. Beans and whole peas can be sprouted before cooking for added value. Liquefy the sprouts with an onion or slice of leek, and vegetable seasoning for taste. Use a vegetable broth or herb tea for the base. Blend smooth and heat to serving point in a double boiler. If you wish, thicken slightly by adding flaxseed meal or a little rice polishings. Just before serving, whisk in some butter or cream.

BEET POTATO SOUP   SERVES 2

1 cup sliced, cooked beets
½ small onion
2 tsp. vegetable seasoning
¼ tsp. paprika
2 Tbs. lemon juice
1 medium-sized potato, unpeeled and cooked
1 cup vegetable broth
1 cup sour cream
1 cup cracked ice
Chopped, fresh dill (as garnish)

1. Begin blending the first six ingredients.
2. Gradually add vegetable broth, sour cream, and ice. Blend thoroughly.
3. Garnish with dill and serve cold.

CAULIFLOWER SOUP   SERVES 2

1 cauliflower, or 1 pkg. frozen cauliflower, broken up
1 cup boiling vegetable broth
1 Tbs. butter
½ tsp. vegetable seasoning
⅛ tsp. nutmeg
½ medium-sized, sliced onion
¼ tsp. cayenne pepper
½ cup cooked potato, cubed
1 cup milk or fresh cream
Parsley (as garnish), or grated Swiss or Gruyère cheese

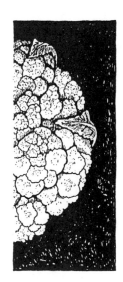

1. Simmer first seven ingredients gently for about five minutes.
2. Place in blender, and begin blending, gradually adding potato and milk or cream.
3. Serve chilled with parsley, or heat to serving point, sprinkle each serving with cheese, and melt cheese under broiler. (Be sure to use heat-proof soup dishes!)

SERVES 3-4

Swiss Chard Soup
A La Liquefier

1 cup steamed Swiss chard
2 tsp. vegetable seasoning
1 tsp. kelp powder (optional)
½ onion, sliced
½ green pepper, sliced
1 or 2 fresh herbs
½ cup mint tea (or another of your own choosing)
2 cups fresh milk
½ cup fresh cream
½ cup French Dressing (page 71)
2 Tbs. grated Romano cheese

1. Blend all ingredients (except Romano cheese) in liquefier.
2. When consistency is smooth, heat in a double boiler to serving temperature.
3. Stir in Romano cheese and serve. Extra Romano cheese sprinkled on top makes a nice garnish.

SERVES 2-3

Cottage Cheese Soup

2 cups vegetable broth or herb tea
½ onion, sliced
Garden cress (or your favorite herb)
2 tsp. vegetable seasoning
½ tsp. dulse powder
½ cup cottage cheese
Fresh cream (if desired)

1. Bring vegetable broth (or herb tea) to a boil.
2. Blend next five ingredients with boiling broth or tea.
3. Add a little cream, if desired. Serve in hot bowls.

LIMA-SESAME SOUP

SERVES 4

1½ cups fresh or frozen green lima beans
2 cups vegetable broth
1 cup thick Sesame Seed Milk (page 103)
½ tsp. dill weed
1 tsp. vegetable seasoning
Lemon, thinly sliced (as garnish)
Paprika (as garnish)

1. Cook beans in broth for five minutes. Set aside.
2. Put heated Sesame Seed Milk, dill seed, and vegetable seasoning in a pre-heated liquefier.
3. Add the beans and mix until smooth.
4. Serve immediately in hot soup bowls, garnishing each with lemon slices and a dash of paprika.

POTATO SOUP

SERVES 4-6

3 large potatoes, sliced
2 onions, sliced
1 bay leaf
2 celery stalks, chopped
1 carrot, sliced
1 Tbs. butter
2 tsp. vegetable seasoning
¼ tsp. paprika
6 sprigs parsley
Hot milk (if thinning is necessary)

1. Cook first five ingredients in water (enough to cover) until tender. Remove bay leaf.
2. Blend in a pre-heated blender, adding butter, vegetable seasoning, paprika, and parsley.
3. Add hot milk, if thinning is necessary.
4. Serve in hot soup dishes.

SERVES 2

POTATO AND PARSLEY BROTH

2 cups diced, unpeeled potatoes
1 cup parsley
1 cup oat straw tea
1-2 tsp. vegetable seasoning
Milk (to correct consistency)
Butter

1. Blend first four ingredients together until smooth.
2. Simmer in a saucepan for a few minutes; add milk.
3. Just prior to serving, add a little butter.

SERVES 3-4

VEGETABLE BROTH DELIGHT

1 cup okra, cut up
1 cup string beans, cut up
1 clove garlic
½ cup celery, cut up
½ cup carrots, cut up
1 large onion, cut up
2 turnips, cut up
½ cup peas
1 pint tomato juice
1 Tbs. vegetable seasoning
Fresh cream (optional)

1. Put cut vegetables (except peas) in a liquefier. Run until finely chopped.
2. Place blended mixture in a pot. Add peas, and steam until tender.
3. Add tomato juice and vegetable seasoning.
4. Re-blend if a smoother soup is desired.
5. A little cream may be added at the table.

''Knowledge is proud that he has learn'd so much;
Wisdom is humble that he knows no more.''

Split Pea Soup.

''You can have anything you want in life;
but you have to take what comes with it.''

Bean-Tomato Soup With Melted Cheese and Red Pepper Garnish.

BLENDED CREAM SOUPS

BASIC RECIPE
SERVES 2-3

2 cups vegetable stock, or vegetable broth
1 Tbs. arrowroot powder
2 Tbs. soft butter
1 tsp. vegetable seasoning
1 thin slice of onion
3 sprigs of parsley
¼ cup celery leaves
1 or 2 cups of a vegetable of your choice
1 cup fresh cream

1. Blend all ingredients (except cream) together until smooth.
2. Place blended mixture in a pot, and stir while cooking over low heat until soup has simmered for about five minutes.
3. Warm the cream (but do not boil).
4. Add warm cream to soup at table, just prior to eating. Stir to blend.

CREAM OF ALMOND SOUP
SERVES 3-4

½ onion, sliced
½ clove garlic
1 fresh bay leaf
1 Tbs. almond butter
1 Tbs. fresh cream
1 Tbs. honey
1 tsp. vegetable seasoning
2½ cups mint tea or water
4 sliced, ripe tomatoes

1. Place first seven ingredients in a pre-heated blender.
2. Bring mint tea (or water) and tomatoes to a boil.
3. Pour boiling mixture over ingredients in blender. Blend until very smooth.
4. Serve immediately in hot bowls.

SERVES 2

CREAM OF ASPARAGUS SOUP

2 cups fresh asparagus pieces (or frozen asparagus)
1/2 cup vegetable broth
Milk (to correct consistency)
1 Tbs. butter
Vegetable seasoning (to taste)
6 sprigs of parsley
Paprika (as garnish)

1. Cook asparagus in broth until tender. Blend smooth in a liquefier.
2. Gradually add milk, butter, vegetable seasoning, and parsley, with blender running.
3. When parsley is chopped, re-heat to serving temperature in a double boiler.
4. Garnish with a sprinkling of paprika upon serving.

SERVES 4

CREAM OF BROCCOLI SOUP

1 small stalk of celery and leaves, chopped
1 medium-sized onion, chopped
1 medium-sized carrot, chopped
1 clove of garlic
1/2 cup oat straw tea
2 cups cooked broccoli, roughly cut
1 tsp. vegetable seasoning
Pinch of cayenne pepper
1/2 cup cooked whole wheat macaroni
1 cup vegetable broth
1/2 cup fresh cream or milk

1. Place first five ingredients in a covered saucepan, bring to a boil, and simmer for ten minutes.
2. Place mixture in a liquefier. Add next four ingredients, and blend.
3. Add next two ingredients, and blend.
4. Serve warm or cold.

CREAM OF LEEK SOUP

SERVES 4-6

2 bunches leeks (lower part only), sliced
2 cups thinly-sliced potato, unpeeled
1 stalk celery (with top), sliced
2 Tbs. finely-chopped parsley
4 cups vegetable broth
1 vegetable bouillon cube
4 tsp. vegetable seasoning
1 cup milk or fresh cream
1 Tbs. sour cream
Dash of nutmeg

1. Bring first seven ingredients to a boil. Simmer until tender.
2. Blend milk or cream (warmed), sour cream, and nutmeg until smooth.
3. Gradually stir this mixture into vegetable broth.
4. Serve in hot soup bowls, or chill and serve as a cold soup.

CREAM OF MUSHROOM SOUP

SERVES 2

1/2 cup water
1 1/2 cups sliced mushrooms
1/2 small onion, sliced
2 cloves garlic
2 tsp. vegetable seasoning
1/2 tsp. paprika
1/2 cup fresh cream
1/2 cup fresh milk

1. Cook first six ingredients gently until tender.
2. Add fresh cream and milk. Blend until smooth.
3. Heat in a double boiler until warm, and serve.

SERVES 2

CREAMED PEA SOUP

1½ cups fresh or frozen green peas
1 cup broth or water
1 bay leaf
¼ tsp. thyme
2 tsp. vegetable seasoning
1 Tbs. butter
1 cup hot milk

1. Combine first four ingredients and cook until tender. Remove bay leaf.
2. Blend until smooth.
3. Add vegetable seasoning, butter, and hot milk, and blend.
4. Serve in hot soup bowls.

SERVES 4

CREAM OF WATERCRESS

2 Tbs. butter
3 Tbs. arrowroot
4 cups milk
1 Tbs. vegetable seasoning
1 bunch watercress
Garlic powder

1. Melt butter over low heat.
2. Add arrowroot, and continue cooking over low heat for three to five minutes, stirring constantly.
3. Stir milk in slowly, creating a white sauce. Stir in vegetable seasoning.
4. Place watercress in a liquefier with sauce and blend until smooth.
5. Place soup in double boiler, and heat to serving temperature.
6. Season with garlic powder, and serve.

BLENDED, RAW SOUPS

CREAMED ASPARAGUS SOUP   SERVES 2

12 young asparagus spears, chopped
1 cup boiling mint tea or water
1-2 cloves garlic, chopped
4 sprigs of mint
2 tsp. vegetable seasoning
Shake of dulse
½ cup skim milk powder or soy milk powder
1½ Tbs. vegetable oil

For a variation, you might try substituting corn (off the cob) for the asparagus.

1. Blend first seven ingredients in a pre-heated liquefier until smooth.
2. With the motor still running, add vegetable oil.
3. Serve in hot soup bowls.

AVOCADO SOUP   SERVES 2

2 cups vegetable broth
1 sliced avocado
2 tsp. vegetable seasoning
2 Tbs. chopped nuts
½ cup fresh cream

1. Boil vegetable broth.
2. Place broth, avocado, and vegetable seasoning, in a pre-heated blender. Blend until smooth.
3. In separate bowl, stir nuts into cream.
4. Place soup in hot bowls, garnishing with cream and nut mixture.

SERVES 2

BEET BORSCH SOUP

1 cup diced raw beets
¾ cup diced raw carrot
¼ cup diced cucumber
1 small onion, sliced
1 cup diluted beet juice or vegetable broth
1 Tbs. lemon juice
1 tsp. raw sugar
Dash of celery salt
Dill (to taste)
1 tsp. vegetable seasoning
Sliced cucumber (as garnish)
Dill (as garnish)
Sour cream or plain yogurt (as garnish)

1. Blend first ten ingredients, adding more liquid if necessary.
2. Serve cold, garnishing with additional slices of cucumber, dill, and spoonfuls of sour cream or yogurt.

SERVES 2

VITAL BEET BORSCH

1 cup diced raw beets
½ small onion, sliced
1 small apple, sliced
1 Tbs. lemon juice
1 tsp. vegetable seasoning
1 tsp. raw sugar
Dash of celery salt
1 cup plain yogurt
½ cup fresh cream
Milk (for thinning)
Sour cream (as garnish)
Sliced cucumber (as garnish)

1. Blend first nine ingredients until smooth and satiny.
2. Add milk to thin (if necessary).
3. Heat to serving temperature or serve cold.
4. Garnish with sour cream and sliced cucumber.

FRESH CORN SOUP

SERVES 2

1½ cups corn (off the cob)
2-3 leaves basil
1½ tsp. vegetable seasoning
1½ cups fresh cream

This soup is excellent for those on a bland diet; corn may be strained to remove hulls.

1. Blend all ingredients until very smooth.
2. Warm if desired.

SWEET CORN CREAM SOUP

SERVES 2

1½ cups corn (off the cob)
2 cups milk or fresh cream
1 slice of onion
1 tsp. vegetable seasoning
Dash of paprika
Butter
Chopped parsley (as garnish)

If a bland soup is desired, corn may be sieved to remove hulls.

1. Blend first five ingredients until very smooth.
2. Heat to serving temperature.
3. Prior to serving, add a pat of butter and sprinkle with chopped parsley.

SERVES 2

CARROT MILK SOUP

³/₄ cup chopped carrots
1¹/₂ cups fresh milk
3 tsp. vegetable seasoning
Shake of cinnamon or nutmeg
Fresh parsley (as garnish)

1. Blend first four ingredients to a smooth cream.
2. Add a little parsley, blend briefly, and serve.

SERVES 2

CREAM OF CELERY SOUP

1¹/₂ cups vegetable broth
³/₄ cup chopped celery
2-3 nasturtium or sorrel leaves
1 Tbs. cashew nuts
2 tsp. vegetable seasoning
1 Tbs. butter
¹/₂ cup fresh cream

1. Blend first five ingredients until smooth.
2. Heat until serving temperature is reached.
3. Add butter and cream, and serve.

SERVES 2

CUCUMBER SOUP

1 cup pineapple juice
1 cup celery juice
1 tsp. plain gelatin
1¹/₂ cups diced cucumber
1 slice of onion
1 sprig of parsley
1 tsp. vegetable seasoning
Fresh cream (as garnish)
Paprika (as garnish)

1. Blend first seven ingredients thoroughly.
2. Serve cold with cream and paprika as garnish.

COOL CUCUMBER SOUP

SERVES 3-4

2 cups cold mint tea or water
2 cloves garlic, chopped fine
Juice and rind of 1 lemon
2 tsp. vegetable seasoning
1 cucumber, sliced
1/2 cup mint leaves
2 Tbs. olive oil
2 cups plain yogurt
1/3 cup currants
Paprika (as garnish)

1. Blend first six ingredients until cucumber has been chopped.
2. Blend in olive oil and yogurt.
3. Stir in currants.
4. Serve chilled, with a garnish of paprika.

SOUR CREAMED CUCUMBER SOUP

SERVES 3-4

1 unpeeled cucumber, chopped
1 3/4 cups thick almond milk
1 tsp. celery salt
Dash of cayenne
1/2 tsp. poultry herbs
1 cup sour cream
Chopped parsley or chives (as garnish)

1. Blend first six ingredients until smooth.
2. Serve chilled, garnishing with chopped parsley or chives.

SERVES 2

FRESH PEA SOUP

½ cup fresh or frozen (uncooked) peas
1 cup vegetable broth or water
1 sprig of mint
1 tsp. vegetable seasoning
½ tsp. raw sugar
2 Tbs. fresh cream

1. Liquefy all ingredients until very smooth.
2. Serve cold or hot.

SERVES 2

SOY MILK CREAMED GREENS

1 cup soy milk
A healthy bunch of spinach, kale, and other green leaves
Vegetable oil (to taste)
Vegetable seasoning (to taste)

1. Heat soy milk in a double boiler.
2. Place soy milk and greens in blender, and liquefy for two or three seconds.
3. Add oil and vegetable seasoning.
4. Serve hot.

SERVES 2

CREAMED GREEN ONION SOUP

1 bunch green onions (with tops), chopped
2 cups vegetable broth
2 mock chicken bouillon cubes
1 cup sour cream (as garnish)
Paprika (as garnish)

1. Combine onions, vegetable broth, and bouillon cubes. Simmer for eight to ten minutes.
2. Place mixture in blender, and liquefy until smooth.
3. Serve in hot bowls, garnishing each dish with ½ cup sour cream and paprika.

SPANISH SOUP

SERVES 2

½ small onion
1 clove garlic
½ green pepper, chopped
3 ripe tomatoes, chopped
1 small cucumber, unpeeled and sliced
1 tsp. vegetable seasoning
¼ tsp. cayenne pepper
2 Tbs. olive oil
3 Tbs. lemon juice
½ cup ice water
Rye bread croutons (page 101)

1. Blend first ten ingredients until all of cucumber has been blended in.
2. Chill. Serve with croutons.

SUMMER PEPPER SOUP

SERVES 2

1 cup celery juice
½ cup pineapple juice, unsweetened
½ cup diced sweet green pepper
1 small tomato, sliced
2 tsp. plain gelatin
Fresh whipped cream or sour cream (as garnish)

1. Blend first five ingredients in a liquefier until smooth.
2. Pour into chilled serving dishes, garnishing each with a spoonful of whipped cream or sour cream.

SERVES 2

TOMATO CREAM SOUP

6 ripe tomatoes, chopped
3 sprigs of parsley
1 tsp. raw sugar
2 slices of onion
1/2 tsp. vegetable seasoning
Dash of lemon juice
Sprinkle of cloves
Fresh cream or milk (to correct consistency)

1. Blend all ingredients until smooth.
2. Heat thoroughly. Add cream or milk to correct consistency.

SERVES 2

TOMATO GREEN SOUP

4 tomatoes, sliced
1/2 cup alfalfa leaves
1 Tbs. chopped onion
1 clove garlic, chopped
3/4 cup milk
1/2 tsp. dulse
3 tsp. vegetable seasoning
1 sprig of mint
2 Tbs. fresh cream

1. Place first eight ingredients in a liquefier and blend until very smooth.
2. Heat in a double boiler until hot.
3. Serve immediately, stirring a tablespoon of cream into each serving.

CREAM OF WATERCRESS SOUP

SERVES 2-4

A healthy bunch of watercress
1 Tbs. arrowroot
2 cups vegetable broth
1 cup fresh cream
Fresh whipped cream (as garnish)
Paprika (as garnish)

1. Blend first three ingredients until watercress is finely chopped.
2. Put in saucepan, and heat to serving temperature.
3. Warm cream, and stir into mixture.
4. Garnish each dish with a spoonful of whipped cream and a dash of paprika.

"JIFFY" SOUPS

When you don't have the time to gather and prepare ingredients for a slowly-simmered soup, here are a few "jiffy" soups that are tasty, hearty, and energizing. A blender is a blessing for those in a hurry, and blenderized soups are easily digested as well as enjoyable. Although I don't recommend hurrying through any meal, when you're on the go and have to beat the clock, my "jiffy" soup recipes can make life a whole lot easier.

JIFFY BROTH

SERVES 1

1 tsp. vegetable seasoning
1 Tbs. whey powder
1 cup boiling water
Chopped parsley (as garnish)

1. Whisk ingredients together.
2. Garnish with a little chopped parsley, if desired.

SERVES 1

JIFFY TOMATO BROTH

2 tsp. vegetable seasoning
1 cup tomato juice
Fresh cream or butter (as garnish)

1. Stir seasoning into tomato juice, and bring mixture to a boil.
2. Serve garnished with cream or butter.

SERVES 2

VITALITY CREAM SOUP

1½ cups milk
3 tsp. arrowroot
Dash of vegetable seasoning
2 tsp. butter
1 cup beet and carrot juice

1. Stir arrowroot and vegetable seasoning into milk. Heat, but do not boil.
2. Add butter and beet and carrot juice. Serve immediately in hot soup dishes.

SERVES 2

BLENDED JIFFY SOUP

½ onion, chopped
1 carrot, chopped
Vegetable seasoning (to taste)
2 cups hot milk or broth

1. Blend all ingredients in a pre-heated blender until smooth.
2. Place in hot dishes and serve.

QUICK VITAL SOUP

SERVES 2

1 small carrot
½ celery stalk
1 slice of onion
1 tsp. vegetable seasoning
Dash of powdered dulse
1 Tbs. soaked nuts
2 Tbs. skim milk powder
½ Tbs. butter
1 cup boiling mint tea

1. Chop first three ingredients, and place in a pre-heated blender.
2. Add remaining ingredients and blend until smooth.
3. Serve immediately in hot soup dishes.

HASTY BLENDED SOUP

SERVES 2

1 cup cooked vegetables (of your own choosing)
¼ onion, sliced
Vegetable seasoning (to taste)
Herbs (of your own choosing)
1 cup broth, milk, or fresh cream (to correct consistency)
Butter (optional, as garnish)
Chopped parsley (optional, as garnish)

1. Blend first five ingredients until smooth.
2. Heat in a double boiler.
3. If desired, add a pat of butter and a sprinkle of chopped parsley upon serving.

PEANUT BUTTER SOUP

SERVES 1

1 cup hot tomato juice
2 Tbs. peanut butter
1 Tbs. fresh cream

1. Stir peanut butter into juice.
2. Serve in a hot soup dish with a spoonful of cream.

THERAPEUTIC SOUPS

Although all properly prepared soups help to promote good health, some soups are especially effective in alleviating specific physical ailments.

Generally, therapeutic soups work by neutralizing acids in the body, by taking care of nutritional deficiencies, by stimulating the elimination channels, and by raising the energy level. One or a combination of the preceding processes are stimulated by what I call a therapeutic soup. The following soups are particularly potent, and I've used them in my practice for many years—with thousands of patients.

SERVES 4

VITAL BROTH

2 cups carrot tops, finely chopped
3 cups celery stalk, finely chopped
2 cups beet tops, finely chopped
2 cups potato peels (cut half an inch thick)
2 cups celery tops, finely chopped
1 tsp. vegetable seasoning
2 qts. distilled water
Carrot or onion (for flavoring, if desired)

This broth neutralizes acidic conditions in the body and may be given to either children or adults for any catarrhal condition or at the onset of any disease or ailment.

1. Combine all ingredients in a large cooking pot.
2. Bring slowly to a boil. Simmer for about twenty minutes.
3. Strain and serve.

VEAL JOINT BROTH

SERVES 4

1 fresh, uncut veal joint
1½ cups apple peels (cut half an inch thick)
2 cups potato peels (cut half an inch thick)
1 small celery stalk
½ cup okra, fresh or canned; or 1 tsp. powdered okra
1 large parsnip
2 beets
1 onion
½ cup parsley

This sodium-rich broth is excellent for joint, gland, ligament, and digestive disorders, and helps to retain youth.

1. Cut up vegetables finely.
2. Wash veal joint in cold water and place in a large saucepan. Cover halfway with water.
3. Add remainder of ingredients.
4. Simmer for four or five hours; strain off broth and drink hot or warm. Refrigerate unused portions.

POTATO PEELING BROTH

SERVES 4

2 large potatoes
4 diced carrots
8 diced celery stalks
A handful of parsley
1½ qts. water

This alkalinizer is excellent for uric acid, kidney, and stomach disorders, and for mineral replacement. (For an irritated stomach, add powdered okra.)

1. Peel potatoes into ¾-inch-thick pieces. Discard centers.
2. Combine all ingredients and simmer for twenty minutes.
3. Strain off liquid and drink as a broth.

POTASSIUM BROTH

SERVES 1

12 sun-dried olives
1 pint boiling water
2 cups potato broth or celery juice

This broth is excellent for heart conditions and digestive disorders, for building muscles and skin, and for healing sores.

1. Steep olives in boiling water for ten minutes.
2. Strain through five or six thicknesses of cheesecloth to eliminate any oil. Discard olives.
3. Add either potato broth or celery juice, if desired.

FISH BROTH

SERVES 4

Fresh fish bones, including head (1½-2 lb. fish)
2 Tbs. powdered celery
¼ tsp. powdered chili
2 Tbs. powdered onion
2 Tbs. vegetable seasoning

This iodine- and phosphorus-rich broth is excellent for the nervous system and the glands. It may also be beneficial during periods of chronic fatigue or mental exhaustion.

1. Simmer fish bones for thirty minutes, adding remainder of ingredients for flavor.
2. Strain off liquid and drink as a broth.

EGGSHELL BROTH

SERVES 1

3 fresh, clean eggshells (crushed)
Distilled water (enough to cover shells)
½ cup goat milk or parsley juice or ½ cup organic orange juice

This calcium broth is excellent for bones and teeth.

1. Cover eggshells with distilled water and simmer slowly over very low heat for fifteen minutes. Strain.
2. Add other high-calcium foods such as goat milk or parsley juice. Or mix half a cup of broth with half a cup of organic orange juice.

CALCIUM BROTH

SERVES 4

½ cup powdered eggshell or chicken bones (or a combination of both)
2 qts. water
Raw celery juice (to taste)

This broth is excellent for strong bones and muscle tone.

1. Boil eggshell or chicken bones in water for thirty to sixty minutes.
2. Strain and drink as a broth, adding celery juice for flavor.

POTATO MILK SOUP

SERVES 1

1 small potato
1 cup milk

This soup is good for diarrhea.

1. Peel potato, cut into pieces, and boil in milk until tender.
2. Rub through a sieve or blend until smooth. Add more boiled milk, if necessary.

BARLEY AND GREEN KALE SOUP

SERVES 2-4

½ cup barley
1 qt. water
2 celery stalks, finely chopped
1 onion, finely chopped
2-3 cups kale, finely chopped
2 tsp. vegetable seasoning
A handful of finely-chopped parsley
Pats of butter
Fresh cream (to taste)

This soup promotes strong bones and teeth, and helps to increase the rate of healing.

1. Soak barley (covered in water) overnight.
2. Add water, celery, and onion. Bring to a boil and simmer for forty minutes.
3. Add kale and vegetable seasoning and cook for another twenty minutes.
4. Upon serving, add parsley, butter, and cream.

CLAM CONSOMME

SERVES 2

2 cups unsalted clam juice
1 cup tomato juice
1 Tbs. lemon juice
1 tsp. onion juice
½ tsp. celery salt
1 tsp. vegetable seasoning
Dash of paprika

This soup is high in iodine.

1. Beat all ingredients together.
2. Serve cold or warm.

RAW VEGETABLE SOUPS

CUCUMBER TOMATO SOUP SERVES 2

2 cups finely-puréed tomato
½ unpeeled cucumber, finely grated
1 green onion, finely chopped
½ cup sour cream
1 tsp. vegetable seasoning
Milk (for thinning)

1. Blend all ingredients until smooth, thinning with milk if necessary.
2. Chill before serving.

SUMMER SOUP SERVES 2

1 cup tomato juice
6 Tbs. lemon juice
6 Tbs. virgin olive oil
1 clove garlic, crushed
2 tsp. vegetable seasoning
4 large, ripe tomatoes, peeled and diced
1 large cucumber, peeled and diced
1 minced onion
Oven-baked croutons (page 101)

1. Thoroughly combine first five ingredients.
2. Add tomatoes, cucumber, and onion, and mix well.
3. Serve with croutons.

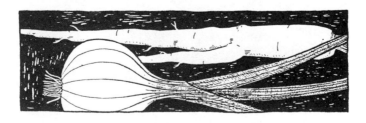

SERVES 4

TOMATO AVOCADO SOUP

1 avocado, mashed
½ cup milk or soy milk
1 qt. tomato juice
Vegetable salt (to taste)
Chopped chives (as garnish)

1. Add milk or soy milk gradually to avocado.
2. Add tomato juice and vegetable salt. Mix until smooth.
3. Heat. Serve with chopped chives.

RAW FRUIT SOUPS

SERVES 2

COOL APPLE SOUP

2 cups Nut Milk (page 103)
2 finely-grated apples
2 tsp. plain gelatin
Honey (for sweetening)
1 Tbs. grape concentrate
Juice and rind of one lemon
Ground cloves (as garnish)

1. Beat first six ingredients together until well blended.
2. Serve cool with a shake of ground cloves.

PEPPERMINT SOUP

SERVES 2

1 cup unsweetened pineapple juice
1 cup strong mint tea
2 tsp. plain gelatin
1 very ripe banana, mashed to a liquid
1 Tbs. apple concentrate
1 Tbs. peppermint leaves, finely chopped
2 lemon wedges (as garnish)

1. Beat first six ingredients together until well blended.
2. Serve cool with a wedge of lemon in each bowl.

COOL AVOCADO SOUP

SERVES 2

1 large avocado, mashed smooth
1½ cups vegetable broth
1 clove garlic, minced fine
⅛ tsp. cayenne pepper
1 tsp. vegetable seasoning
½ cup fresh cream
½ cup milk
Dill (as garnish)

1. Beat first seven ingredients together until well blended.
2. Serve cool with a sprinkling of dill.

6. *HERBS FOR SOUPS AND SALADS:*
Adding Zest to Your Creations

The purpose of adding herbs to soups and salads is to balance their flavor and nutritional value. Whether you are making your soup or salad from scratch or re-heating yesterday's leftovers, herbs will add color and zest. You can even bring your own herbs to the local salad bar and add them at the table. Of course, it's much easier to add herbs to salads at home. Because herbs are usually rich in specific vitamins, minerals, volatile oils, enzymes, and other nutrients, they enhance the nutritional value of any salad or soup.

Herbal flavors are usually improved in soups if added the day before and refrigerated overnight. In general, flavoring herbs should be added at the beginning of soup preparation, while nutrient herbs (like fresh parsley) should be added when the soup is nearly done. Of course, chopped chives or parsley can be stirred in or sprinkled on top of just about any kind of soup.

Salads—whether green, egg, or potato—are a challenge to the imagination and creativity of anyone who likes to use herbs for flavoring. So be adventurous! Your salads will be more colorful, more flavorful, and—best of all—more healthful.

WHAT DO FRESH HERBS TASTE LIKE?

Many people are reluctant to use herbs because they aren't sure what they will taste like. While words can never fully describe the actual taste of an herb, here are some hints for those who have never sampled the following fresh herbs:

- *Lovage* tastes a little bit like celery.
- *Coriander* (cilantro) has a cool, pungent flavor.
- *Burnet* tastes like fresh cucumber.
- *Marjoram* is pungent.
- *Dill weed* is both sweet and mildly pungent.
- *Anise leaves* provide a light, sweet licorice flavor.

If this doesn't tempt your taste buds, I highly recommend sampling the real thing!

HERBS IN SOUPS

I recommend the following herbs for soups: angelica seeds, basil, bay, burnet, chervil, chives, coriander leaves, costmary, dill, French sorrel, garlic, lovage, marjoram, parsley, rosemary, sage, savory, sweet cicely, tarragon, and thyme.

Growing Your Own Herbs

Herbs are used to spark the taste of foods and to enhance their nutritional value. Although dry herbs can be used when fresh are not available, you'll find that fresh herbs are more flavorful. As an added bonus, fresh herbs are higher in nutrients and, of course, make beautiful garnishes.

While some supermarkets now carry fresh herbs, the best way to insure a handy supply is to grow the herbs yourself. Because herbs adapt well to most conditions, they can be grown almost anywhere—in a rock garden, in pots on your window sill or patio, or in hanging baskets; among your flowers and vegetables, or in a separate herb garden; in sunny conditions, or, in the case of some herbs, in shade.

If you have room, you'll be able to grow a wide variety of herbs. Popular ones include parsley, chives, tarragon, basil, rosemary, thyme, sage, marjoram, and dill, to name just a few. If space is limited, though, you'll probably want to grow only your favorite herbs, or only those most commonly used. Parsley, for instance, is a good choice, being useful both as a garnish and as flavoring.

Light conditions, too, may limit your choice of herbs. Most herbs will do best in a sunny spot, but some—mint and angelica, for instance—will thrive in shade or partial shade.

Your local nursery may carry a number of herbs as potted plants. If they don't have what you want, though, you'll be able to grow most herbs from seeds. A few, such as tarragon, must be grown from cuttings. Once you've decided what plants you want

to grow, check with your nursery to find the proper source.

Seeds can be sown directly in the garden (during warm weather only, of course), or can be germinated indoors or outdoors in pots or flats, and transplanted later on. If planting seeds in the garden, first turn the soil and break up any large lumps of earth. If planting in pots, use a light potting soil. After sowing, keep the soil moist, and shelter it from direct sunlight. For best results, follow the directions on the seed packet. The seed packet will also tell you when you can expect to see the first plants breaking through the soil.

Seedlings may be thinned and transplanted as soon as they look hardy. (Again, check the seed packet for specific directions.) If moving the plants outdoors, wait until the weather is warm and mild. Seedlings are fragile, and cannot survive direct sunlight, cold temperatures, or heavy rains.

When your herbs are mature and strong, you'll be able to start snipping leaves off for use in your kitchen. Herbs planted in pots need more water than herbs planted in the ground, so if you're using pots—whether indoors or out—check the soil frequently and add water whenever the soil seems dry. Unless you are growing the herbs for flowers or seeds as well as leaves, cut off the flowering tops as they appear; this will make the plant fuller and healthier. To keep the plants attractive as well as useful, pick a little from each side so that they remain thick and bushy. With proper care, your plants will thrive, and your family will be able to enjoy dishes that are tasty, attractive, and nutritious.

Suggestions for herbal use in particular soups include:

- *Cream soups*—¼ cup each of finely-chopped fresh parsley and chives per quart of soup
- *Chicken soup*—fresh coriander (cilantro) to taste
- *Clam chowder*—pinch of thyme per quart
- *Crab bisque*—bay leaf, 1 tsp. parsley, ½ tsp. thyme per quart
- *Fish chowder*—costmary
- *French onion*—¼ tsp. oregano, ½ tsp. parsley per quart
- *Potato soup*—1 tsp. parsley, ¼ tsp. sage per quart
- *Tomato soup*—basil

Fines herbes is a French term for a finely-chopped combination of herbs. Here's a good "fines herbes" for soups: parsley, chervil, tarragon, and chives. Always be sure to use fresh herbs, not dry ones.

HERBS IN SALADS

There's a great herbal combination you can add to any tossed green salad. If you can get all fresh herbs, finely chop up one cup of tarragon and one cup of parsley, and mix thoroughly with one-fourth cup each of finely-chopped oregano, celery leaves, and dill. Keep in an airtight jar with a lid. It doesn't keep for more than a few days, so be careful.

Another nice "fines herbes" combination for salads can be made from one teaspoon each of marjoram, basil, and vegetable seasoning, and one tablespoon each of parsley, tarragon, and grated lemon rind. These should be mixed together thoroughly.

Individual herbs that work well in salads include anise, basil, borage (leaves and flowers), chervil, chives, young comfrey leaves, coriander leaves (cilantro), costmary, cress, fennel, garlic, fresh gotu kola, marjoram, mint, parsley, savory, French sorrel, lemon-scented thyme, sweet violet (leaves and flowers), and watercress.

Some more specific herbs for salads include:

- burnet leaves for egg salad
- lemon verbena or licorice mint for fruit salad
- dill weed for chicken salad
- tarragon for shrimp salad
- chopped chives and dill weed for potato salad
- oregano for tuna salad

Herb lovers say that the best vinegar to use in salad dressings is herb vinegar, made by steeping a sprig of fresh herb in pure apple cider

vinegar. This herb may be tarragon, burnet, basil, dill, or another of your choice.

Following is a favorite recipe of many herb lovers. Be sure to use all fresh herbs!

MAKES 1 CUP

HERB SALAD DRESSING

1 clove garlic
1 Tbs. chopped basil
1 Tbs. chopped chives
1 Tbs. chopped parsley
1 Tbs. chopped chervil
³/4 cup olive oil
¹/4 cup herb vinegar

1. Combine ingredients together in a jar and shake well.
2. Refrigerate overnight.

A Closing Thought

Both soups and salads are universally enjoyed, not only as delicious additions to any menu, but also as builders of health. When made lovingly and with only the freshest ingredients, soups and salads are low in calories, and high in minerals, vitamins, and much-needed fiber.

In this book, I have offered you new taste experiences from around the country and around the world. My goal has been to show you the many delicious ways in which soups and salads can lead you to greater well-being. It is my hope that this book will be a jumping-off place, and that you will experiment to find your own ways of using nature's bounty to enliven your menu and improve your health.

So eat right and feel good! Become the person you would really like to be—full of vigor and life. Best of health!

Index

About the Author

Bernard Jensen was born March 25, 1908, in Stockton, California. Following in his father's footsteps, he entered the West Coast Chiropractic College in Oakland, California at the age of 18. Shortly after his graduation, his health failed. Doctors diagnosed the problem as bronchiectasis, a severe and often fatal lung condition for which there was no known cure. He was told that medical science could offer him no hope.

Unwilling to give up, young Dr. Jensen sought the help of a Seventh-Day Adventist physician who taught him the basics of proper nutrition, pulled him off all "junk" foods, and placed him on a natural food diet. Improvement was slow, but steady. As a result of a breathing exercise program developed by Thomas Gaines, he added four inches to his chest in a year's time. Because nature offered him a cure when medical science could do nothing, Dr. Jensen determined to learn all he could about natural healing.

His training included postgraduate courses at the National Chiropractic College in Chicago, Illinois. Later, Dr. Jensen returned to California to study iridology, the science of interpreting tissue conditions from the iris, with Dr. R.M. McClain at the International School of Arts and Sciences in San Francisco, California.

To expand his knowledge of health work, Dr. Jensen studied bowel care with Dr. John Harvey Kellogg of Battle Creek, Michigan, and Dr. Max Gerson of New York, the latter known for his use of nutrition, diets, supplements, and enemas in the treatment of degenerative disease. Among others, Dr. Jensen also studied with Dr. O.B. Shellberg of New York, a colonics specialist; Dr. Ralph Benner, of the Bircher-Benner Clinic in Switzerland; Dr. John Tilden of Denver, Colorado, and Dr. George Weger of Redlands, California.

Dr. Jensen operated several health sanitariums in California, the first in Ben Lomond, the second at Alta Dena, and the last at Escondido. It is this last sanitarium that he refers to as "the Ranch." At the sanitariums, he lived with his patients day in and day out. "The sanitarium was my university," Dr. Jensen says, "and my patients were my books." The sanitariums were living laboratories where he was able to observe first-hand what best brought patients back to health.

Over the years, Dr. Jensen has received many honors and awards, including Knighthood in the Order of St. John of Malta; the Dag Hammarskjöld Peace Award of the Pax Mundi Academy in Brussels, Belgium; and an award from Queen Juliana of the Netherlands for his nutritional work. In 1982, he received the National Health Federation's Pioneer Doctor of the Year award.

At the age of 76, Dr. Jensen earned his Ph.D. from the University of Humanistic Studies in San Diego, California, climaxing a lifetime of study, work, and teaching in the healing arts. He has lectured in 55 countries around the world and has authored over 40 books on the subjects of natural health care and iridology.

Now in his eighties, Dr. Jensen continues to write, lecture, travel, and learn.

If You've Enjoyed Reading This Book . . .

. . . why not tell a friend about it? If you're interested in learning more about Dr. Bernard Jensen's approach to health, here are some other titles you may find to be informative, engaging, and fun.

Vibrant Health From Your Kitchen

A warm and wonderful tour through Dr. Jensen's latest discoveries about food, nutrition, and health, this book provides the guidance needed to keep your family disease-free, healthy, and happy.

Tissue Cleansing Through Bowel Management

Toxin-laden tissue can become a breeding ground for disease. This remarkable book instructs you in the removal of toxins and the restoration of health and youthfulness through the cleansing and care of the organs of elimination.

Food Healing for Man

We now know that foods can repair the tissue damage that accompanies most illness and disease. Look over the shoulders of the great pioneer nutritionists as they investigate the links between nutrition and disease.

Chlorella: Gem of the Orient

Why does Dr. Jensen consider chlorella—a green alga—the most valuable broad-spectrum food supplement discovery of the twentieth century? You'll find out in this unusually beautiful, fully illustrated, hard cover book.

Creating a Magic Kitchen

This is Dr. Jensen's introductory primer on the art of selecting and preparing foods for the best of health. Short, easy to understand, and handy to use, this is the perfect book for anyone who wants a more healthful and enjoyable lifestyle.

Nature Has a Remedy

This popular classic provides a delightful description of the many paths to natural healing—foods, herbs, exercise, climate selection, personology, and hundreds of effective remedies.

World Keys to Health and Long Life

Based on Dr. Jensen's travels to over fifty-five countries, this fascinating book describes the health and longevity secrets of centenarians interviewed in the Hunza Valley of India; Vilcabamba, Peru; the Caucasus Mountains of the Soviet Union; and other places around the world.

Doctor–Patient Handbook

Discover the reversal process and healing crisis that Nature uses to rid the body of disease and restore well-being. Here is a fresh approach to wholistic health.

Slender Me Naturally

Dr. Jensen's answer to fad diets that don't work is a natural weight loss program that does. Developed over fifty-eight years of experience with overweight patients, this program is a healthful and effective way of losing unwanted weight.

Breathe Again Naturally

Get rid of asthma, allergies, bronchitis, hay fever, and other respiratory problems. Dr. Jensen discusses nutrition, herbs that work, food supplements, breathing exercises, attitude, and climate.

Arthritis, Rheumatism and Osteoporosis

Are you among the one in four Americans who suffers from arthritis, rheumatism, or osteoporosis? Would you like to know what to do about it? This book is for you.

Foods That Heal

This book presents the basic principles of Hippocrates, Dr. Rocine, and Dr. Jensen regarding the use of foods to help the body regain health. The author has also included a complete guide to the various fruits and vegetables we all need.

In Search of Shangri-La

Here is the very personal journal of Dr. Jensen's physical and spiritual travels through China into Tibet, and his reflections on his search for Shangri-La.

Beyond Basic Health

Dr. Jensen looks at the deteriorating state of modern man's health and offers practical advice and insights to those health professionals who must deal with today's devastating illnesses.

Love, Sex and Nutrition

Based on years of detailed study, this book explores the link between diet, sensuality, and relationships. This is an important and practical guide for people who wish to improve their sexuality safely and naturally.

For information regarding prices, write to:

Hidden Valley Health Ranch
24360 Old Wagon Road
Escondido, California 92027